DAILY PLANNER
for a
GREAT LIFE

CLAUDIA WILLIAMS

WESTBOW
PRESS®
A DIVISION OF THOMAS NELSON
& ZONDERVAN

WestBow Press books may be ordered through booksellers or by contacting:

WestBow Press
A Division of Thomas Nelson & Zondervan
1663 Liberty Drive
Bloomington, IN 47403
www.westbowpress.com
844-714-3454

ISBN: 978-1-6642-0790-5 (sc)
ISBN: 978-1-9736-9832-6 (e)

Print information available on the last page.

WestBow Press rev. date: 11/19/2020

INTRODUCTION

God gives us two gifts: the first is life, and the second is a chance for a great life. The difference between a good life and a great life depends on how we spend each precious minute.

God gives us a special assignment, something no one else is in the position to fill. We are equipped with unique gifts and talents designed for our specific calling. Imagine crossing a bridge that leads to the extraordinary life and purpose God has created for you. On one side of the bridge is unfulfilling idleness. Doing nothing in life is sinful, a waste. On the other side of the bridge is meaningless frenzy. Life is so busy and overwhelming that we are incapable of meeting all its demands. Hurrying through the day is just as wasteful as doing nothing! Is it any wonder then that Satan works so hard to throw into our heads ideas that lead us to chase relentlessly after selfish ambition? Likewise, it is no surprise that the enemy tries to lead us astray in isolation, emptiness, and destruction. Satan works hard to keep us closed within ourselves and separate from the abundant life God wants to give us. Don't get lost on the roads to idleness and frenzy. God has provided a compass to remain on the narrow path towards the extraordinary life He created for each of us.

Let's face it. We don't know how to live. We must be trained, and Jesus is the teacher. Jesus desires a life that is beneficial for us and His kingdom. A life centered in Christ keeps us from wandering in the wrong direction. Psalm 90:12 reminds us to desire knowledge about spending time wisely. Scripture says, "Teach us to number our days, that we may gain a heart of wisdom." Proverbs 3:5–6 instructs us to "Trust in the Lord with all your heart and lean not on your understanding; in all your ways submit to Him, and He will make your paths straight." The choice is clear. Put God first.

As worthy as all other concerns may be, the moment they become the focus of our efforts, they become idolatry. Life-changing transformation takes place when we acknowledge God and follow Him. Nature provides examples. Consider a caterpillar that breaks free from its self-absorbed cocoon to be transformed into spectacular beauty. If the splendor of a transformed worm is significant to God, how much more does He desire for you to escape your limitations? Acknowledge God, and cooperate with His excellent plan. Be transformed into the miraculous creation God intended. Awaken to a deeper dimension of freedom, and discover a world full of opportunities unimagined.

WORSHIP: DRAW CLOSER TO THE KING OF KINGS

First things, first! Being a good steward of time requires first, to remember who we are in Christ and second, to consult with the King of glory on managing His affairs. Start each day in the presence of our King! Make time on purpose to rest in the presence of the Almighty! We can't live powerfully and effectively if we keep constantly on the go. Placing God above all else is a choice. Don't work God into your schedule. Work your schedule around God. Focus and search for the holiness of Jesus within. Have this singleness of purpose in mind, with no distractions. Release all cares to Him. Let all tension melt away. Soak in the presence and love of God. Rest in Him! This is holy leisure!

Spend time to reflect on who God is, not what He can do for you. What do you admire about Him? Can you truly fathom the extent of His existence? He is the Alpha and Omega. He is the beginning and end. He is the Creator who speaks all things into existence. His majesty extends beyond this world and this universe. His character is full of light; there is no darkness in Him. He is pure love, goodness, faithfulness, kindness, gentleness, self-control, faithfulness, peace, and patience. Consider His radiance! His majesty! His omnipotence! His holiness! His truth! His beauty! Spend time in awe of Him. Soak in all that He is, and be immersed in His presence. During this time, express reverence and adoration only for Him. During this time, there is no room for personal petitions. Seek the giver, not the gift. Just want more of Him.

Miracles are phenomena derived only through faith and occur during worship. The transforming power of worship should be no surprise for anyone who has opened him- or herself to the adventurous life God has planned. To stand in the radiant glory of the Holy One of eternity is to be changed. The Virgin Mary, upon learning she was carrying the baby Jesus, said, "From now on all generations will call me blessed, for the Mighty One has done great things for me—holy is his name" (Luke 1:48–49). What a miracle that after 2,000 years, Mother Mary is still called "blessed." When faith is at the center of one's life, the power of the Holy Spirit is increased, and miracles happen.

Worship includes freedom to express adoration and to hear from God in many forms. Sit in silence immersed in the radiance and peace of His glorious presence. Experience how the words and melody of gospel music can soften a heart for the love of God. Walk and observe the splendor and beauty of all His creation. Acknowledge God's goodness in all of nature: enjoy the fragrance of flowers, the song of birds, and the warmth of midday sun. You can worship sitting down, standing up, kneeling, or lying prostrate on the floor. What's important is taking time to draw closer to Him. Praise Him for who He is.

Draw closer to God through scripture. Find a quiet place for this sacred moment. Ask for God's grace to keep Jesus as the teacher. Invoke His presence by proclaiming faith in Him. Learn about Him. Learn about God's Word, which is full of grace. This grace is the power of the Holy Spirit. Keep a teachable heart by studying with a spirit of humility. Repeat scripture, memorize it, and use it as a mantra. Pray scripture back to God. Consider God's perspective. Apply what you are reading to personal experiences. *Daily Devotions for a Great Life* complements this planner with daily devotion, prayer, and additional scripture reading for each day's topic. Replace one of the character's names in scripture with your own, and use all five senses of sight, smell, taste, hearing, and touch to make the gospel more meaningful. Reading and repeating scripture is an excellent way to get God's Word moved from one's mind and absorbed in one's heart.

Bible study is also an excellent way to worship. Being focused on God's perception on topics of importance perpetuates insight and godly reflection. Even when bombarded with problems of the world, keep a Bible near, and stay focused on the Holy Spirit. Question and evaluate, seeking proper perspective and guidance.

Fellowship was a form of worship practiced much more extensively by early Christians. Today the importance of fellowship is often overlooked, and the precepts are often misunderstood. For a deeper and more meaningful appreciation for this form of worship, Dietrich Bonhoeffer wrote an excellent source of practical advice in *Life Together*. The Bible is bursting with scripture on its necessity, which is just as applicable today as it was for the early church. The benefits and purpose of fellowship include the following:

- Be of one mind. Be in harmony with one another of faith, united in praising and honoring God.
- Love one another. Loving others involves listening with compassion and patience. Show hospitality, and bear one another's burdens.
- Build one another up. As iron sharpens iron, we sharpen one another. Through fellowship, we teach, guide, correct, grow, and strengthen one another. Administer to others' needs, listen to their perspectives, and encourage their spiritual gifts. No one can hear the whole counsel of God in isolation.
- Be separated from darkness. Be separated from anyone or anything immoral, negative, or divisive. Keep away from pride, lust, greed, idolatry, or any other form of darkness.
- Strengthen the body of Christ. Be champions of faith through godly living. We are in relationship to do good work and share our faith. Together we can accomplish anything.

PURE HEART

Consider the purity of God. Before the grace and power of the Holy Spirit can be accessed, we must create a heart sanctuary. No evil thing can stand in His presence. God can't exist where there is darkness. Finite humans need purity to engage in divine dialogue. Proverbs 4:23 reminds us to guard our hearts, for from the heart flows everything of life. A heart that seeks hard after God and hates sin clears a way to hear from God. A heart filled with light delights in His presence. Only then can the throne of grace be accessed and power in prayer be increased.

Unconfessed sin separates us from God and His abundant blessing. Pray Psalm 139:23–24 to God. "Search me, God, and know my heart; test me and know my anxious thoughts. See if there is any offensive way in me, and lead me in the way everlasting." Ask God to reveal anything that grieves the Holy Spirit. Meditate deeper on Philippians 4:8: "Finally, brothers and sisters, whatever is true, whatever is noble, whatever is right, whatever is pure, whatever is lovely, whatever is admirable—if anything is excellent or praiseworthy—think about such things." Inward reflection and introspection lead to confession. Confession is all God needs to reveal His splendor! There is celebration in the forgiveness of sins because it results in access to the divinity of God's redeeming power. Fear nothing but sin, and seek nothing but God.

THANKFULNESS

The nature of God is joy! Celebration is central to the gospel. Jesus spread joy in His coming and going. Angels exclaimed the good news and great joy of the birth of Christ (Luke 2:10)! When Jesus departed, He told His disciples, "I have told you this so that my joy may be in you and that your joy may be complete" (John 15:11). The Israelites were commanded to gather to celebrate the goodness of God. There is great joy in being transformed into the image, character, and calling of God. There is incredible joy in responding to the liberating touch of the Holy Spirit. Sanctifying ordinary daily life with a spirit of service is a divinely appointed cause for celebration. Nehemiah 8:10 confirms that "the joy of the Lord is your strength!" Joy brings strength, refreshment, and energy!

No wonder the enemy works so hard to steal our joy! Don't be an easy target. Joy is a choice! The devil throws his best shots to take our joy, hope, and faith in all of God's promises. Confound that old devil and remind him that troubles are temporary; turn every care over to God, who fights every battle. Don't give power to the enemy and dwell on offenses! Instead, avoid these traps and take negative thoughts captive! Come to the throne of grace with praise and thanksgiving. Walking with God is fullness of joy. Be free of care! Joy sustains us! Trust and praise God! Turn all anxiety over to Him. Then go about enjoying life! That is God's anointed path to freedom. Every day, decide to celebrate! Punctuate every minute with inward breathings of joy! Meditate on that, and do it on purpose!

Thankfulness is spiritual warfare! Be thankful, and say so! Every day, write down at least three things to be thankful for and revisit them for encouragement. On particularly troublesome days, stop immediately and take ten! Stop and think of ten things at that moment to be grateful for. What a blessing it is to have clean water and a place to sleep at night. See incredible beauty in God's creation. Thank God for all that He is and all that He has done. Name them one by one: all the seemingly coincidental events, miracles, and blessings! Write them down, and revisit them often! Tell others how good God is! Keep the enemy from stealing what is rightfully yours! Keeping a joyful and thankful heart is the key to enter the gates of the great Almighty.

REFLECTION: GOD'S PERSPECTIVE AND ETERNAL SIGNIFICANCE

God wants to "feed you" with His Word. Reflect on God's Word and how the passages relate to life. Take a small piece of God's Word, and chew it slowly for its transformative effect. Consider how scripture improves perspective, attitude, and life. Imagine Him high and lifted up. As you do, listen for that still, small voice and hear affirmations for changed behavior and renewed strength. Imagine Him lovingly walking beside you throughout the day!

There is divine mystery in everything. Reflect on what influences people, including their likes and dislikes, and what makes them different. Consider each person's God-given character and qualities and their eternal significance. How do people manage relationships and family?

Reflect on financial stewardship. Everything belongs to God, but we are managers of what He has provided. Good managers can be trusted with more. God wants us to experience great joy and prosperity but won't give us more if it destroys us. There are two tests in life concerning money. The first is how you behave and manage when you have money. The second is how you behave and manage when you don't have money. God wants us to have abundance, but He does not want us to serve it. God promises that if we seek the kingdom first, all these things will be given to us. Seek the Giver, not the gift!

Are you a slave for more? Craving more is bondage. God loves you so much that He wants you to be satisfied with what you have. When is enough enough? Is there anything so important you can't live without it? How easy is it to let go of coffee in the morning? Are cravings controlling you, or are you controlling them? Let go of anything that holds power over you for a week and see!

Reflect on work. Many people work hard to climb the corporate ladder only to find their ladder is leaning against the wrong building. Some people don't know how to manage authority. Some people laud power over others rather than using it to help, guide, and build others up. Some rely on a job to determine their self-worth and value, but true worth and value come from who we are in Christ. Status can be valuable for servant-leadership, but all too often it is used for one's own personal power and recognition. No one can respect a prideful, self-indulgent leader—not employees, not supervisors, and certainly not God.

Time is a precious commodity. A daily to-do list becomes an idol if it is the primary focus for the day! Busyness is self-adoration. Being joyfully indifferent when everything isn't completed reflects an inward spirit of trust in the One who matters most. Reflect on how you can better manage your time.

There is freedom in serving. Sacrificing for others frees us from self-pity, self-indulgence, and always having to have our way. Setting proper limits to submission is equally essential to consider. Jesus requires a full understanding of our infinite worth (Matthew 22:39). Children of God are treasures not to be trampled on. Doing for others what they should do for themselves is sin. God loves the cheerful giver. When giving is no longer a cheerful endeavor, it may be a sign that a season of giving has come to an end. Think also about accepting service. Not allowing others to sow into your life may be a sign of pride keeping you from God's best! Matthew 5:37 warns us to guard our hearts by letting our yes be yes and our no mean no. Anything more is evil. God's chosen are set free from serving under guilt or obligation and from being objects of others' games for power or promotion. We are warned against seeking recognition for services. When our service becomes an idol, it replaces true worship and is sin. In Genesis, God told Abraham to leave his family because there was a different season of service. So how is the proper perspective on who, what, when, and where to serve distinguished? Setting rigid rules and unhealthy boundaries is not the answer. Follow peace; follow the promptings of the Holy Spirit. The Spirit alone is the accurate discerner.

Are your emotions in check? Is there an attitude that needs to be adjusted? Are you called to be more sensitive to others, or do you need to demonstrate more tough love? Do you refuse to approve every whim? Ask God to show you perfect joy.

Spending sacred time with God is an opportunity to seek guidance and prioritize the ministry He predestined for each believer. Ecclesiastes 7:29 says, "God created mankind upright, but they have gone in search of many schemes." God made life so sweet and simple, but we tend to complicate it. Finish your race so that when all is said and done, our Father in Heaven will celebrate with "Well done, good and faithful servant" (Matthew 25:21). Reflect on these things, and ask God for proper perspective, priorities, and boundaries.

REVELATION: PRACTICE LISTENING FOR GOD

Psalm 85:8 reminds us to listen with expectancy to what God says. Christ is alive and present in all His power. He wants to reveal unfathomable things you do not know. He wants to reveal a life overflowing with joy! Revelation is divine insight received from the profound experience of being in God's presence. Divine promptings come in many forms. Guidance can be revealed in flashes of thought about things forgotten or left undone. Feelings emerge, urging us to guard our hearts and minds. Hearing the name of a loved one may prompt us to reach out or pray for him or her. Even seemingly coincidental events can change the course of our lives and set us off in a new direction.

Ask God for discernment. God's voice can be heard, and His presence can be made known in our hearts. The blessings God wants to provide His children are treasures too extraordinary to miss. Submitting to God's perfect will is liberating! It is freedom! What is producing joy in your life? What is beneficial? What is adding value? Refuse to be a slave to anything but God! He guides us and delights in showing us a better way. Submit to the King of Glory, who prepares us for every good thing. He wants to teach us, guide us, rebuke us, and comfort us. Stay immersed in the Holy Spirit to gain a clearer understanding of God's will. What has God placed on your heart? Where is He leading you?

OBEDIENCE: STAND, SHARE, SERVE, AND TAKE STEPS OF FAITH

All of God's creation has a purpose. You are divinely appointed to take care of His sheep! Divine obedience is a choice. Does someone need love, a smile, or words of encouragement? The Bible reminds us that faith without works is dead. You are a unique masterpiece designed to do good works for the kingdom. You are commissioned to share the good news, build into others' lives, and promote a higher way of thinking. The Holy Spirit leads the way a person lives if he or she genuinely seeks, obeys, and trusts in God. The level of miracles is directly dependent on the level of obedience. When prompted to act, do something immediately!

PRAYER AND FASTING: YOU HAVE NOT BECAUSE YOU ASK NOT

Why pray? First and foremost, God wants a personal, intimate relationship with us. Prayer is a pleasant conversation with our best friend, the King of the universe. Stay attuned to the divine. He invites us to share our joy and our cares. Imagine Jesus with you at work, while fixing dinner, driving, or sitting in front of the TV. Listen for His voice instructing, guiding, and caring about every moment of the day. The power of prayer is enhanced by remaining in the perpetual presence of our Lord.

Pray for others, with others, and do it unceasingly throughout the day. Pray standing up, sitting down, or lying prostrate on the floor. Pray while walking the dog; pray while eating. Pray first thing in the morning and last thing at night. Pray that God abides in your coming and going. Pray that He fills your heart, your home, and your future. As you read scripture, pray it back to God. Pray to release anxiety! As you pray, wait patiently for His way to be manifest! What a privilege to come before God in prayer.

When you pray, believe! Stand on the promises of His Word. Mark 11:24 requires absolute belief in what is prayed for. When prayers are not answered in the way or time hoped for, trust Him. That's the faith God seeks. Sometimes God needs us to know something first before He answers prayer. God looks for a heart that trusts, endures, and seeks after Him. God is good no matter what. In His presence is fullness of joy. Trust that in His mercy, He will bring one hundredfold for what is best.

Lastly, fasting is a form of prayer, but it's not as widely practiced today as it was in the days of Jesus. Jesus never said, "If you fast." But in Matthew 6:16–18, Jesus said, "When you fast." His instruction indicates that fasting is something we should be doing. There is tremendous merit in fasting. It brings breakthroughs in the spiritual realm that can't be experienced any other way. It's a means to take authority in prayer life by taking authority over what controls you. It's an open-door invitation to learn the perfect will of God. A fast is a very personal and sacred time with the Lord. Fasts honor God, and only you and God may know the outcome or resulting benefit.

There are many ways to fast. Scripture emphasizes that our food is a tool for fasting. As such, a fast may be a partial or whole fast. Abstain from a meal, refrain from fish on Fridays, or resist desserts for a week. A fast could be providing a sacred service to the Lord or meeting a personal challenge. Motives are important to God. Fasting to try to get a desired result from God is cheap grace. Attention should not be brought to what you are doing. Fasting is an opportunity and not a law, as the Pharisees required. And lastly, fasting should never be used to inflict harm or punishment. Isaiah 58 is an excellent resource for gaining knowledge about fasting. For further insight into the purpose, method, and benefits of fasting, read *The Essential Guide to Fasting* by Elmer L. Towns.

Fasting is spiritual warfare and is Christ-focused. The weapons of war are described in Ephesians 6:10–17: "Be strong in the Lord and in His mighty power. Put on the full armor of God." We are encouraged to stand against the devil's schemes to derail us by putting on the full armor of God. Stand firm in truth, righteousness, and readiness with the gospel of peace. Take up the shield of faith and the Word of God, knowing that we have salvation through Christ. Be a prayer warrior!

Your life matters to God! Make God the priority of your life. Put Him on the throne! Live the abundant life God created for you. Don't let the devil rob you of what is rightfully yours! Fight the good fight of faith! Stay grounded in the Word! Keep abiding in His love! "Always give yourselves fully to the work of the Lord, because you know that your labor in the Lord is not in vain" (1 Corinthians 15:58).

JANUARY

_____
_____
_____
_____
_____
_____

FEBRUARY

_____
_____
_____
_____
_____
_____

MARCH

_____
_____
_____
_____
_____
_____

APRIL

_____
_____
_____
_____
_____
_____

MAY

_____
_____
_____
_____
_____
_____

JUNE

_____
_____
_____
_____
_____
_____

JULY

_____
_____
_____
_____
_____
_____

AUGUST

_____
_____
_____
_____
_____
_____

SEPTEMBER

_____
_____
_____
_____
_____
_____

OCTOBER

_____
_____
_____
_____
_____
_____

NOVEMBER

_____
_____
_____
_____
_____
_____

DECEMBER

_____
_____
_____
_____
_____
_____

MONTH:

SUNDAY	MONDAY	TUESDAY	WEDNESDAY	THURSDAY	FRIDAY	SATURDAY

PLACES TO GO, PEOPLE TO SEE, THINGS TO DO:

MONTHLY GOALS	STEPS OF FAITH	MONTHLY GOALS	STEPS OF FAITH

MONTH:

SUNDAY	MONDAY	TUESDAY	WEDNESDAY	THURSDAY	FRIDAY	SATURDAY

PLACES TO GO, PEOPLE TO SEE, THINGS TO DO:

MONTHLY GOALS	STEPS OF FAITH	MONTHLY GOALS	STEPS OF FAITH

MONTH:

SUNDAY	MONDAY	TUESDAY	WEDNESDAY	THURSDAY	FRIDAY	SATURDAY

PLACES TO GO, PEOPLE TO SEE, THINGS TO DO:

MONTHLY GOALS	STEPS OF FAITH	MONTHLY GOALS	STEPS OF FAITH

MONTH:

SUNDAY	MONDAY	TUESDAY	WEDNESDAY	THURSDAY	FRIDAY	SATURDAY

PLACES TO GO, PEOPLE TO SEE, THINGS TO DO:

MONTHLY GOALS	STEPS OF FAITH	MONTHLY GOALS	STEPS OF FAITH

MONTH:

SUNDAY	MONDAY	TUESDAY	WEDNESDAY	THURSDAY	FRIDAY	SATURDAY

PLACES TO GO, PEOPLE TO SEE, THINGS TO DO:

MONTHLY GOALS	STEPS OF FAITH	MONTHLY GOALS	STEPS OF FAITH

MONTH:

SUNDAY	MONDAY	TUESDAY	WEDNESDAY	THURSDAY	FRIDAY	SATURDAY

PLACES TO GO, PEOPLE TO SEE, THINGS TO DO:

MONTHLY GOALS	STEPS OF FAITH	MONTHLY GOALS	STEPS OF FAITH

WEEKLY FOCUS

Last Week's Reflection
Areas to Celebrate:
Areas to Improve:
What did I learn

This Week's Planning
Plan for joyful occasions. Joy is your strength, refreshment, energy, and beauty. What are you looking forward to this week? Find something to laugh about and share it.

Projects/Areas of focus this week:

- [ ]
- [ ]
- [ ]
- [ ]
- [ ]
- [ ]
- [ ]

AREAS TO SIMPLIFY – where to set godly boundaries

	What is important	What is not important	Why	What are Facts/Feelings	Benefits of continuing/not continuing	Pray about possibilities and solutions
Time						
Energy						
Money						
Relationships						
Possessions						

FASTING: Take authority over what controls me; lean on God; keep Christ-focused
What to fast:
Time to fast:
How to fast:
Check motives:

ADDITIONAL REFLECTION

Date:

SCRIPTURE – DRAW CLOSER TO THE KING OF KINGS: Use your name in the place of a character in the scripture you're reading; imagine yourself in that time, using all 5 senses. Pray scripture back to God. Write the scripture down, read it, repeat it out loud throughout the day, memorize it, and meditate on it.

WORSHIP – PRAISE HIM FOR WHO HE IS: How will you glorify and magnify Him today? There is no room here for making personal petitions.

PURE HEART – ASK HIM TO PURIFY YOUR MIND AND HEART: Replace negative thoughts with higher thoughts. God's thoughts are noble, pure, lovely, excellent, right, true, and admirable. Ask God to reveal areas in your life that grieve the Holy Spirit. Confess with a contrite heart and receive forgiveness. As you confess, turn your palms up and release your sin, worry, and anxiety over to God. Now turn your palms down and receive God's love, mercy, favor, and grace.

THANKFULNESS – NAME THOSE THINGS YOU ARE THANKFUL FOR: There's always something to be grateful for. Name them one by one and come back often to rekindle the joy of each one of them.

O

O

O

O

O

O

O

	TASKS
REFLECTION & REVELATION – PRACTICE LISTENING FOR GOD: God promises that if you draw near to Him, He will tell you things you do not know. Who does God bring to mind? Where is God leading you? Reflect on God's perspective.	
PRAYER – YOU HAVE NOT BECAUSE YOU ASK NOT: Pray for family, friends, relationships, unity, community, world, church, favor, wisdom, God's will, work, and your future. Pray about anything and everything, without ceasing.	
OBEDIENCE – STAND, SHARE, SERVE: Take steps of faith, and obey promptly. The level of miracles in your life will be directly related to your level of obedience. Faith without works is dead. You have an assignment, a destiny to fulfill.	
	6 am
	7 am
	8 am
	9 am
	10 am
	11 am
	12 pm
	1 pm
	2 pm
	3 pm
	4 pm
	5 pm
	6 pm
	7 pm
	8 pm
	9 pm

Date:

SCRIPTURE – DRAW CLOSER TO THE KING OF KINGS: Use your name in the place of a character in the scripture you're reading; imagine yourself in that time, using all 5 senses. Pray scripture back to God. Write the scripture down, read it, repeat it out loud throughout the day, memorize it, and meditate on it.

_____
_____
_____
_____
_____
_____
_____
_____
_____
_____
_____
_____
_____
_____
_____

WORSHIP – PRAISE HIM FOR WHO HE IS: How will you glorify and magnify Him today? There is no room here for making personal petitions.

_____
_____
_____
_____

PURE HEART – ASK HIM TO PURIFY YOUR MIND AND HEART: Replace negative thoughts with higher thoughts. God's thoughts are noble, pure, lovely, excellent, right, true, and admirable. Ask God to reveal areas in your life that grieve the Holy Spirit. Confess with a contrite heart and receive forgiveness. As you confess, turn your palms up and release your sin, worry, and anxiety over to God. Now turn your palms down and receive God's love, mercy, favor, and grace.

_____
_____
_____

THANKFULNESS – NAME THOSE THINGS YOU ARE THANKFUL FOR: There's always something to be grateful for. Name them one by one and come back often to rekindle the joy of each one of them.

O

O

O

O

O

O

O

REFLECTION & REVELATION – PRACTICE LISTENING FOR GOD: God promises that if you draw near to Him, He will tell you things you do not know. Who does God bring to mind? Where is God leading you? Reflect on God's perspective.	TASKS
PRAYER – YOU HAVE NOT BECAUSE YOU ASK NOT: Pray for family, friends, relationships, unity, community, world, church, favor, wisdom, God's will, work, and your future. Pray about anything and everything, without ceasing.	
OBEDIENCE – STAND, SHARE, SERVE: Take steps of faith, and obey promptly. The level of miracles in your life will be directly related to your level of obedience. Faith without works is dead. You have an assignment, a destiny to fulfill.	
	6 am
	7 am
	8 am
	9 am
	10 am
	11 am
	12 pm
	1 pm
	2 pm
	3 pm
	4 pm
	5 pm
	6 pm
	7 pm
	8 pm
	9 pm

Date:

SCRIPTURE – DRAW CLOSER TO THE KING OF KINGS: Use your name in the place of a character in the scripture you're reading; imagine yourself in that time, using all 5 senses. Pray scripture back to God. Write the scripture down, read it, repeat it out loud throughout the day, memorize it, and meditate on it.

WORSHIP – PRAISE HIM FOR WHO HE IS: How will you glorify and magnify Him today? There is no room here for making personal petitions.

PURE HEART – ASK HIM TO PURIFY YOUR MIND AND HEART: Replace negative thoughts with higher thoughts. God's thoughts are noble, pure, lovely, excellent, right, true, and admirable. Ask God to reveal areas in your life that grieve the Holy Spirit. Confess with a contrite heart and receive forgiveness. As you confess, turn your palms up and release your sin, worry, and anxiety over to God. Now turn your palms down and receive God's love, mercy, favor, and grace.

THANKFULNESS – NAME THOSE THINGS YOU ARE THANKFUL FOR: There's always something to be grateful for. Name them one by one and come back often to rekindle the joy of each one of them.

O

O

O

O

O

O

O

REFLECTION & REVELATION – PRACTICE LISTENING FOR GOD: God promises that if you draw near to Him, He will tell you things you do not know. Who does God bring to mind? Where is God leading you? Reflect on God's perspective.	TASKS
PRAYER – YOU HAVE NOT BECAUSE YOU ASK NOT: Pray for family, friends, relationships, unity, community, world, church, favor, wisdom, God's will, work, and your future. Pray about anything and everything, without ceasing.	
OBEDIENCE – STAND, SHARE, SERVE: Take steps of faith, and obey promptly. The level of miracles in your life will be directly related to your level of obedience. Faith without works is dead. You have an assignment, a destiny to fulfill.	
	6 am
	7 am
	8 am
	9 am
	10 am
	11 am
	12 pm
	1 pm
	2 pm
	3 pm
	4 pm
	5 pm
	6 pm
	7 pm
	8 pm
	9 pm

Date:

SCRIPTURE – DRAW CLOSER TO THE KING OF KINGS: Use your name in the place of a character in the scripture you're reading; imagine yourself in that time, using all 5 senses. Pray scripture back to God. Write the scripture down, read it, repeat it out loud throughout the day, memorize it, and meditate on it.

WORSHIP – PRAISE HIM FOR WHO HE IS: How will you glorify and magnify Him today? There is no room here for making personal petitions.

PURE HEART – ASK HIM TO PURIFY YOUR MIND AND HEART: Replace negative thoughts with higher thoughts. God's thoughts are noble, pure, lovely, excellent, right, true, and admirable. Ask God to reveal areas in your life that grieve the Holy Spirit. Confess with a contrite heart and receive forgiveness. As you confess, turn your palms up and release your sin, worry, and anxiety over to God. Now turn your palms down and receive God's love, mercy, favor, and grace.

THANKFULNESS – NAME THOSE THINGS YOU ARE THANKFUL FOR: There's always something to be grateful for. Name them one by one and come back often to rekindle the joy of each one of them.

O

O

O

O

O

O

O

REFLECTION & REVELATION – PRACTICE LISTENING FOR GOD: God promises that if you draw near to Him, He will tell you things you do not know. Who does God bring to mind? Where is God leading you? Reflect on God's perspective.	TASKS
PRAYER – YOU HAVE NOT BECAUSE YOU ASK NOT: Pray for family, friends, relationships, unity, community, world, church, favor, wisdom, God's will, work, and your future. Pray about anything and everything, without ceasing.	
OBEDIENCE – STAND, SHARE, SERVE: Take steps of faith, and obey promptly. The level of miracles in your life will be directly related to your level of obedience. Faith without works is dead. You have an assignment, a destiny to fulfill.	
	6 am
	7 am
	8 am
	9 am
	10 am
	11 am
	12 pm
	1 pm
	2 pm
	3 pm
	4 pm
	5 pm
	6 pm
	7 pm
	8 pm
	9 pm

Date:

SCRIPTURE – DRAW CLOSER TO THE KING OF KINGS: Use your name in the place of a character in the scripture you're reading; imagine yourself in that time, using all 5 senses. Pray scripture back to God. Write the scripture down, read it, repeat it out loud throughout the day, memorize it, and meditate on it.

_____
_____
_____
_____
_____
_____
_____
_____
_____
_____
_____
_____
_____

WORSHIP – PRAISE HIM FOR WHO HE IS: How will you glorify and magnify Him today? There is no room here for making personal petitions.

_____
_____
_____
_____

PURE HEART – ASK HIM TO PURIFY YOUR MIND AND HEART: Replace negative thoughts with higher thoughts. God's thoughts are noble, pure, lovely, excellent, right, true, and admirable. Ask God to reveal areas in your life that grieve the Holy Spirit. Confess with a contrite heart and receive forgiveness. As you confess, turn your palms up and release your sin, worry, and anxiety over to God. Now turn your palms down and receive God's love, mercy, favor, and grace.

_____
_____
_____
_____

THANKFULNESS – NAME THOSE THINGS YOU ARE THANKFUL FOR: There's always something to be grateful for. Name them one by one and come back often to rekindle the joy of each one of them.

O _____

O _____

O _____

O _____

O _____

O _____

O _____

REFLECTION & REVELATION – PRACTICE LISTENING FOR GOD: God promises that if you draw near to Him, He will tell you things you do not know. Who does God bring to mind? Where is God leading you? Reflect on God's perspective.	TASKS
PRAYER – YOU HAVE NOT BECAUSE YOU ASK NOT: Pray for family, friends, relationships, unity, community, world, church, favor, wisdom, God's will, work, and your future. Pray about anything and everything, without ceasing.	
OBEDIENCE – STAND, SHARE, SERVE: Take steps of faith, and obey promptly. The level of miracles in your life will be directly related to your level of obedience. Faith without works is dead. You have an assignment, a destiny to fulfill.	
	6 am
	7 am
	8 am
	9 am
	10 am
	11 am
	12 pm
	1 pm
	2 pm
	3 pm
	4 pm
	5 pm
	6 pm
	7 pm
	8 pm
	9 pm

Date:

SCRIPTURE – DRAW CLOSER TO THE KING OF KINGS: Use your name in the place of a character in the scripture you're reading; imagine yourself in that time, using all 5 senses. Pray scripture back to God. Write the scripture down, read it, repeat it out loud throughout the day, memorize it, and meditate on it.

_____
_____
_____
_____
_____
_____
_____
_____
_____
_____
_____

WORSHIP – PRAISE HIM FOR WHO HE IS: How will you glorify and magnify Him today? There is no room here for making personal petitions.

_____
_____
_____

PURE HEART – ASK HIM TO PURIFY YOUR MIND AND HEART: Replace negative thoughts with higher thoughts. God's thoughts are noble, pure, lovely, excellent, right, true, and admirable. Ask God to reveal areas in your life that grieve the Holy Spirit. Confess with a contrite heart and receive forgiveness. As you confess, turn your palms up and release your sin, worry, and anxiety over to God. Now turn your palms down and receive God's love, mercy, favor, and grace.

_____
_____
_____

THANKFULNESS – NAME THOSE THINGS YOU ARE THANKFUL FOR: There's always something to be grateful for. Name them one by one and come back often to rekindle the joy of each one of them.

O
O
O
O
O
O
O

	TASKS
REFLECTION & REVELATION – PRACTICE LISTENING FOR GOD: God promises that if you draw near to Him, He will tell you things you do not know. Who does God bring to mind? Where is God leading you? Reflect on God's perspective.	
PRAYER – YOU HAVE NOT BECAUSE YOU ASK NOT: Pray for family, friends, relationships, unity, community, world, church, favor, wisdom, God's will, work, and your future. Pray about anything and everything, without ceasing.	
OBEDIENCE – STAND, SHARE, SERVE: Take steps of faith, and obey promptly. The level of miracles in your life will be directly related to your level of obedience. Faith without works is dead. You have an assignment, a destiny to fulfill.	
	6 am
	7 am
	8 am
	9 am
	10 am
	11 am
	12 pm
	1 pm
	2 pm
	3 pm
	4 pm
	5 pm
	6 pm
	7 pm
	8 pm
	9 pm

Date:

SCRIPTURE – DRAW CLOSER TO THE KING OF KINGS: Use your name in the place of a character in the scripture you're reading; imagine yourself in that time, using all 5 senses. Pray scripture back to God. Write the scripture down, read it, repeat it out loud throughout the day, memorize it, and meditate on it.

WORSHIP – PRAISE HIM FOR WHO HE IS: How will you glorify and magnify Him today? There is no room here for making personal petitions.

PURE HEART – ASK HIM TO PURIFY YOUR MIND AND HEART: Replace negative thoughts with higher thoughts. God's thoughts are noble, pure, lovely, excellent, right, true, and admirable. Ask God to reveal areas in your life that grieve the Holy Spirit. Confess with a contrite heart and receive forgiveness. As you confess, turn your palms up and release your sin, worry, and anxiety over to God. Now turn your palms down and receive God's love, mercy, favor, and grace.

THANKFULNESS – NAME THOSE THINGS YOU ARE THANKFUL FOR: There's always something to be grateful for. Name them one by one and come back often to rekindle the joy of each one of them.

O

O

O

O

O

O

O

	TASKS
REFLECTION & REVELATION – PRACTICE LISTENING FOR GOD: God promises that if you draw near to Him, He will tell you things you do not know. Who does God bring to mind? Where is God leading you? Reflect on God's perspective.	
PRAYER – YOU HAVE NOT BECAUSE YOU ASK NOT: Pray for family, friends, relationships, unity, community, world, church, favor, wisdom, God's will, work, and your future. Pray about anything and everything, without ceasing.	
OBEDIENCE – STAND, SHARE, SERVE: Take steps of faith, and obey promptly. The level of miracles in your life will be directly related to your level of obedience. Faith without works is dead. You have an assignment, a destiny to fulfill.	
	6 am
	7 am
	8 am
	9 am
	10 am
	11 am
	12 pm
	1 pm
	2 pm
	3 pm
	4 pm
	5 pm
	6 pm
	7 pm
	8 pm
	9 pm

WEEKLY FOCUS

Last Week's Reflection
Areas to Celebrate:
Areas to Improve:
What did I learn

This Week's Planning
Plan for joyful occasions. Joy is your strength, refreshment, energy, and beauty. What are you looking forward to this week? Find something to laugh about and share it.

Projects/Areas of focus this week:

- [ ]
- [ ]
- [ ]
- [ ]
- [ ]
- [ ]
- [ ]

AREAS TO SIMPLIFY – where to set godly boundaries

	What is important	What is not important	Why	What are Facts/Feelings	Benefits of continuing/not continuing	Pray about possibilities and solutions
Time						
Energy						
Money						
Relationships						
Possessions						

FASTING: Take authority over what controls me; lean on God; keep Christ-focused
What to fast:
Time to fast:
How to fast:
Check motives:

ADDITIONAL REFLECTION

Date:

SCRIPTURE – DRAW CLOSER TO THE KING OF KINGS: Use your name in the place of a character in the scripture you're reading; imagine yourself in that time, using all 5 senses. Pray scripture back to God. Write the scripture down, read it, repeat it out loud throughout the day, memorize it, and meditate on it.

WORSHIP – PRAISE HIM FOR WHO HE IS: How will you glorify and magnify Him today? There is no room here for making personal petitions.

PURE HEART – ASK HIM TO PURIFY YOUR MIND AND HEART: Replace negative thoughts with higher thoughts. God's thoughts are noble, pure, lovely, excellent, right, true, and admirable. Ask God to reveal areas in your life that grieve the Holy Spirit. Confess with a contrite heart and receive forgiveness. As you confess, turn your palms up and release your sin, worry, and anxiety over to God. Now turn your palms down and receive God's love, mercy, favor, and grace.

THANKFULNESS – NAME THOSE THINGS YOU ARE THANKFUL FOR: There's always something to be grateful for. Name them one by one and come back often to rekindle the joy of each one of them.

O

O

O

O

O

O

O

	TASKS
REFLECTION & REVELATION – PRACTICE LISTENING FOR GOD: God promises that if you draw near to Him, He will tell you things you do not know. Who does God bring to mind? Where is God leading you? Reflect on God's perspective.	
PRAYER – YOU HAVE NOT BECAUSE YOU ASK NOT: Pray for family, friends, relationships, unity, community, world, church, favor, wisdom, God's will, work, and your future. Pray about anything and everything, without ceasing.	
OBEDIENCE – STAND, SHARE, SERVE: Take steps of faith, and obey promptly. The level of miracles in your life will be directly related to your level of obedience. Faith without works is dead. You have an assignment, a destiny to fulfill.	
	6 am
	7 am
	8 am
	9 am
	10 am
	11 am
	12 pm
	1 pm
	2 pm
	3 pm
	4 pm
	5 pm
	6 pm
	7 pm
	8 pm
	9 pm

Date:

SCRIPTURE – DRAW CLOSER TO THE KING OF KINGS: Use your name in the place of a character in the scripture you're reading; imagine yourself in that time, using all 5 senses. Pray scripture back to God. Write the scripture down, read it, repeat it out loud throughout the day, memorize it, and meditate on it.

WORSHIP – PRAISE HIM FOR WHO HE IS: How will you glorify and magnify Him today? There is no room here for making personal petitions.

PURE HEART – ASK HIM TO PURIFY YOUR MIND AND HEART: Replace negative thoughts with higher thoughts. God's thoughts are noble, pure, lovely, excellent, right, true, and admirable. Ask God to reveal areas in your life that grieve the Holy Spirit. Confess with a contrite heart and receive forgiveness. As you confess, turn your palms up and release your sin, worry, and anxiety over to God. Now turn your palms down and receive God's love, mercy, favor, and grace.

THANKFULNESS – NAME THOSE THINGS YOU ARE THANKFUL FOR: There's always something to be grateful for. Name them one by one and come back often to rekindle the joy of each one of them.

O

O

O

O

O

O

O

REFLECTION & REVELATION – PRACTICE LISTENING FOR GOD: God promises that if you draw near to Him, He will tell you things you do not know. Who does God bring to mind? Where is God leading you? Reflect on God's perspective.	TASKS
PRAYER – YOU HAVE NOT BECAUSE YOU ASK NOT: Pray for family, friends, relationships, unity, community, world, church, favor, wisdom, God's will, work, and your future. Pray about anything and everything, without ceasing.	
OBEDIENCE – STAND, SHARE, SERVE: Take steps of faith, and obey promptly. The level of miracles in your life will be directly related to your level of obedience. Faith without works is dead. You have an assignment, a destiny to fulfill.	
	6 am
	7 am
	8 am
	9 am
	10 am
	11 am
	12 pm
	1 pm
	2 pm
	3 pm
	4 pm
	5 pm
	6 pm
	7 pm
	8 pm
	9 pm

Date:

SCRIPTURE – DRAW CLOSER TO THE KING OF KINGS: Use your name in the place of a character in the scripture you're reading; imagine yourself in that time, using all 5 senses. Pray scripture back to God. Write the scripture down, read it, repeat it out loud throughout the day, memorize it, and meditate on it.

_____

_____

_____

_____

_____

_____

_____

_____

_____

_____

_____

_____

_____

_____

WORSHIP – PRAISE HIM FOR WHO HE IS: How will you glorify and magnify Him today? There is no room here for making personal petitions.

_____

_____

_____

_____

PURE HEART – ASK HIM TO PURIFY YOUR MIND AND HEART: Replace negative thoughts with higher thoughts. God's thoughts are noble, pure, lovely, excellent, right, true, and admirable. Ask God to reveal areas in your life that grieve the Holy Spirit. Confess with a contrite heart and receive forgiveness. As you confess, turn your palms up and release your sin, worry, and anxiety over to God. Now turn your palms down and receive God's love, mercy, favor, and grace.

_____

_____

_____

THANKFULNESS – NAME THOSE THINGS YOU ARE THANKFUL FOR: There's always something to be grateful for. Name them one by one and come back often to rekindle the joy of each one of them.

O

O

O

O

O

O

O

REFLECTION & REVELATION – PRACTICE LISTENING FOR GOD: God promises that if you draw near to Him, He will tell you things you do not know. Who does God bring to mind? Where is God leading you? Reflect on God's perspective.	TASKS
PRAYER – YOU HAVE NOT BECAUSE YOU ASK NOT: Pray for family, friends, relationships, unity, community, world, church, favor, wisdom, God's will, work, and your future. Pray about anything and everything, without ceasing.	
OBEDIENCE – STAND, SHARE, SERVE: Take steps of faith, and obey promptly. The level of miracles in your life will be directly related to your level of obedience. Faith without works is dead. You have an assignment, a destiny to fulfill.	
	6 am
	7 am
	8 am
	9 am
	10 am
	11 am
	12 pm
	1 pm
	2 pm
	3 pm
	4 pm
	5 pm
	6 pm
	7 pm
	8 pm
	9 pm

Date:

SCRIPTURE – DRAW CLOSER TO THE KING OF KINGS: Use your name in the place of a character in the scripture you're reading; imagine yourself in that time, using all 5 senses. Pray scripture back to God. Write the scripture down, read it, repeat it out loud throughout the day, memorize it, and meditate on it.

WORSHIP – PRAISE HIM FOR WHO HE IS: How will you glorify and magnify Him today? There is no room here for making personal petitions.

PURE HEART – ASK HIM TO PURIFY YOUR MIND AND HEART: Replace negative thoughts with higher thoughts. God's thoughts are noble, pure, lovely, excellent, right, true, and admirable. Ask God to reveal areas in your life that grieve the Holy Spirit. Confess with a contrite heart and receive forgiveness. As you confess, turn your palms up and release your sin, worry, and anxiety over to God. Now turn your palms down and receive God's love, mercy, favor, and grace.

THANKFULNESS – NAME THOSE THINGS YOU ARE THANKFUL FOR: There's always something to be grateful for. Name them one by one and come back often to rekindle the joy of each one of them.

O

O

O

O

O

O

O

REFLECTION & REVELATION – PRACTICE LISTENING FOR GOD: God promises that if you draw near to Him, He will tell you things you do not know. Who does God bring to mind? Where is God leading you? Reflect on God's perspective.	TASKS
PRAYER – YOU HAVE NOT BECAUSE YOU ASK NOT: Pray for family, friends, relationships, unity, community, world, church, favor, wisdom, God's will, work, and your future. Pray about anything and everything, without ceasing.	
OBEDIENCE – STAND, SHARE, SERVE: Take steps of faith, and obey promptly. The level of miracles in your life will be directly related to your level of obedience. Faith without works is dead. You have an assignment, a destiny to fulfill.	
	6 am
	7 am
	8 am
	9 am
	10 am
	11 am
	12 pm
	1 pm
	2 pm
	3 pm
	4 pm
	5 pm
	6 pm
	7 pm
	8 pm
	9 pm

Date:

SCRIPTURE – DRAW CLOSER TO THE KING OF KINGS: Use your name in the place of a character in the scripture you're reading; imagine yourself in that time, using all 5 senses. Pray scripture back to God. Write the scripture down, read it, repeat it out loud throughout the day, memorize it, and meditate on it.

WORSHIP – PRAISE HIM FOR WHO HE IS: How will you glorify and magnify Him today? There is no room here for making personal petitions.

PURE HEART – ASK HIM TO PURIFY YOUR MIND AND HEART: Replace negative thoughts with higher thoughts. God's thoughts are noble, pure, lovely, excellent, right, true, and admirable. Ask God to reveal areas in your life that grieve the Holy Spirit. Confess with a contrite heart and receive forgiveness. As you confess, turn your palms up and release your sin, worry, and anxiety over to God. Now turn your palms down and receive God's love, mercy, favor, and grace.

THANKFULNESS – NAME THOSE THINGS YOU ARE THANKFUL FOR: There's always something to be grateful for. Name them one by one and come back often to rekindle the joy of each one of them.

O

O

O

O

O

O

O

REFLECTION & REVELATION – PRACTICE LISTENING FOR GOD: God promises that if you draw near to Him, He will tell you things you do not know. Who does God bring to mind? Where is God leading you? Reflect on God's perspective.	TASKS
PRAYER – YOU HAVE NOT BECAUSE YOU ASK NOT: Pray for family, friends, relationships, unity, community, world, church, favor, wisdom, God's will, work, and your future. Pray about anything and everything, without ceasing.	
OBEDIENCE – STAND, SHARE, SERVE: Take steps of faith, and obey promptly. The level of miracles in your life will be directly related to your level of obedience. Faith without works is dead. You have an assignment, a destiny to fulfill.	
	6 am
	7 am
	8 am
	9 am
	10 am
	11 am
	12 pm
	1 pm
	2 pm
	3 pm
	4 pm
	5 pm
	6 pm
	7 pm
	8 pm
	9 pm

Date:

SCRIPTURE – DRAW CLOSER TO THE KING OF KINGS: Use your name in the place of a character in the scripture you're reading; imagine yourself in that time, using all 5 senses. Pray scripture back to God. Write the scripture down, read it, repeat it out loud throughout the day, memorize it, and meditate on it.

WORSHIP – PRAISE HIM FOR WHO HE IS: How will you glorify and magnify Him today? There is no room here for making personal petitions.

PURE HEART – ASK HIM TO PURIFY YOUR MIND AND HEART: Replace negative thoughts with higher thoughts. God's thoughts are noble, pure, lovely, excellent, right, true, and admirable. Ask God to reveal areas in your life that grieve the Holy Spirit. Confess with a contrite heart and receive forgiveness. As you confess, turn your palms up and release your sin, worry, and anxiety over to God. Now turn your palms down and receive God's love, mercy, favor, and grace.

THANKFULNESS – NAME THOSE THINGS YOU ARE THANKFUL FOR: There's always something to be grateful for. Name them one by one and come back often to rekindle the joy of each one of them.

O

O

O

O

O

O

O

REFLECTION & REVELATION – PRACTICE LISTENING FOR GOD: God promises that if you draw near to Him, He will tell you things you do not know. Who does God bring to mind? Where is God leading you? Reflect on God's perspective.	TASKS
PRAYER – YOU HAVE NOT BECAUSE YOU ASK NOT: Pray for family, friends, relationships, unity, community, world, church, favor, wisdom, God's will, work, and your future. Pray about anything and everything, without ceasing.	
OBEDIENCE – STAND, SHARE, SERVE: Take steps of faith, and obey promptly. The level of miracles in your life will be directly related to your level of obedience. Faith without works is dead. You have an assignment, a destiny to fulfill.	
	6 am
	7 am
	8 am
	9 am
	10 am
	11 am
	12 pm
	1 pm
	2 pm
	3 pm
	4 pm
	5 pm
	6 pm
	7 pm
	8 pm
	9 pm

Date:

SCRIPTURE – DRAW CLOSER TO THE KING OF KINGS: Use your name in the place of a character in the scripture you're reading; imagine yourself in that time, using all 5 senses. Pray scripture back to God. Write the scripture down, read it, repeat it out loud throughout the day, memorize it, and meditate on it.

_____
_____
_____
_____
_____
_____
_____
_____
_____
_____
_____
_____

WORSHIP – PRAISE HIM FOR WHO HE IS: How will you glorify and magnify Him today? There is no room here for making personal petitions.

_____
_____
_____
_____

PURE HEART – ASK HIM TO PURIFY YOUR MIND AND HEART: Replace negative thoughts with higher thoughts. God's thoughts are noble, pure, lovely, excellent, right, true, and admirable. Ask God to reveal areas in your life that grieve the Holy Spirit. Confess with a contrite heart and receive forgiveness. As you confess, turn your palms up and release your sin, worry, and anxiety over to God. Now turn your palms down and receive God's love, mercy, favor, and grace.

_____
_____
_____

THANKFULNESS – NAME THOSE THINGS YOU ARE THANKFUL FOR: There's always something to be grateful for. Name them one by one and come back often to rekindle the joy of each one of them.

O
O
O
O
O
O
O

	TASKS
REFLECTION & REVELATION – PRACTICE LISTENING FOR GOD: God promises that if you draw near to Him, He will tell you things you do not know. Who does God bring to mind? Where is God leading you? Reflect on God's perspective.	
PRAYER – YOU HAVE NOT BECAUSE YOU ASK NOT: Pray for family, friends, relationships, unity, community, world, church, favor, wisdom, God's will, work, and your future. Pray about anything and everything, without ceasing.	
OBEDIENCE – STAND, SHARE, SERVE: Take steps of faith, and obey promptly. The level of miracles in your life will be directly related to your level of obedience. Faith without works is dead. You have an assignment, a destiny to fulfill.	
	6 am
	7 am
	8 am
	9 am
	10 am
	11 am
	12 pm
	1 pm
	2 pm
	3 pm
	4 pm
	5 pm
	6 pm
	7 pm
	8 pm
	9 pm

WEEKLY FOCUS

Last Week's Reflection
Areas to Celebrate:
Areas to Improve:
What did I learn

This Week's Planning
Plan for joyful occasions. Joy is your strength, refreshment, energy, and beauty. What are you looking forward to this week? Find something to laugh about and share it.
Projects/Areas of focus this week:

- ☐
- ☐
- ☐
- ☐
- ☐
- ☐
- ☐

AREAS TO SIMPLIFY – where to set godly boundaries

	What is important	What is not important	Why	What are Facts/Feelings	Benefits of continuing/not continuing	Pray about possibilities and solutions
Time						
Energy						
Money						
Relationships						
Possessions						

FASTING: Take authority over what controls me; lean on God; keep Christ-focused
What to fast:
Time to fast:
How to fast:
Check motives:

Additional Reflection

Date:

SCRIPTURE – DRAW CLOSER TO THE KING OF KINGS: Use your name in the place of a character in the scripture you're reading; imagine yourself in that time, using all 5 senses. Pray scripture back to God. Write the scripture down, read it, repeat it out loud throughout the day, memorize it, and meditate on it.

WORSHIP – PRAISE HIM FOR WHO HE IS: How will you glorify and magnify Him today? There is no room here for making personal petitions.

PURE HEART – ASK HIM TO PURIFY YOUR MIND AND HEART: Replace negative thoughts with higher thoughts. God's thoughts are noble, pure, lovely, excellent, right, true, and admirable. Ask God to reveal areas in your life that grieve the Holy Spirit. Confess with a contrite heart and receive forgiveness. As you confess, turn your palms up and release your sin, worry, and anxiety over to God. Now turn your palms down and receive God's love, mercy, favor, and grace.

THANKFULNESS – NAME THOSE THINGS YOU ARE THANKFUL FOR: There's always something to be grateful for. Name them one by one and come back often to rekindle the joy of each one of them.

O

O

O

O

O

O

O

REFLECTION & REVELATION – PRACTICE LISTENING FOR GOD: God promises that if you draw near to Him, He will tell you things you do not know. Who does God bring to mind? Where is God leading you? Reflect on God's perspective.	TASKS
PRAYER – YOU HAVE NOT BECAUSE YOU ASK NOT: Pray for family, friends, relationships, unity, community, world, church, favor, wisdom, God's will, work, and your future. Pray about anything and everything, without ceasing.	
OBEDIENCE – STAND, SHARE, SERVE: Take steps of faith, and obey promptly. The level of miracles in your life will be directly related to your level of obedience. Faith without works is dead. You have an assignment, a destiny to fulfill.	
	6 am
	7 am
	8 am
	9 am
	10 am
	11 am
	12 pm
	1 pm
	2 pm
	3 pm
	4 pm
	5 pm
	6 pm
	7 pm
	8 pm
	9 pm

Date:

SCRIPTURE – DRAW CLOSER TO THE KING OF KINGS: Use your name in the place of a character in the scripture you're reading; imagine yourself in that time, using all 5 senses. Pray scripture back to God. Write the scripture down, read it, repeat it out loud throughout the day, memorize it, and meditate on it.

_____
_____
_____
_____
_____
_____
_____
_____
_____
_____
_____
_____

WORSHIP – PRAISE HIM FOR WHO HE IS: How will you glorify and magnify Him today? There is no room here for making personal petitions.

_____
_____
_____
_____

PURE HEART – ASK HIM TO PURIFY YOUR MIND AND HEART: Replace negative thoughts with higher thoughts. God's thoughts are noble, pure, lovely, excellent, right, true, and admirable. Ask God to reveal areas in your life that grieve the Holy Spirit. Confess with a contrite heart and receive forgiveness. As you confess, turn your palms up and release your sin, worry, and anxiety over to God. Now turn your palms down and receive God's love, mercy, favor, and grace.

_____
_____
_____

THANKFULNESS – NAME THOSE THINGS YOU ARE THANKFUL FOR: There's always something to be grateful for. Name them one by one and come back often to rekindle the joy of each one of them.

O
O
O
O
O
O
O

REFLECTION & REVELATION – PRACTICE LISTENING FOR GOD: God promises that if you draw near to Him, He will tell you things you do not know. Who does God bring to mind? Where is God leading you? Reflect on God's perspective.	TASKS
PRAYER – YOU HAVE NOT BECAUSE YOU ASK NOT: Pray for family, friends, relationships, unity, community, world, church, favor, wisdom, God's will, work, and your future. Pray about anything and everything, without ceasing.	
OBEDIENCE – STAND, SHARE, SERVE: Take steps of faith, and obey promptly. The level of miracles in your life will be directly related to your level of obedience. Faith without works is dead. You have an assignment, a destiny to fulfill.	
	6 am
	7 am
	8 am
	9 am
	10 am
	11 am
	12 pm
	1 pm
	2 pm
	3 pm
	4 pm
	5 pm
	6 pm
	7 pm
	8 pm
	9 pm

Date:

SCRIPTURE – DRAW CLOSER TO THE KING OF KINGS: Use your name in the place of a character in the scripture you're reading; imagine yourself in that time, using all 5 senses. Pray scripture back to God. Write the scripture down, read it, repeat it out loud throughout the day, memorize it, and meditate on it.

_____

_____

_____

_____

_____

_____

_____

_____

_____

_____

_____

_____

_____

WORSHIP – PRAISE HIM FOR WHO HE IS: How will you glorify and magnify Him today? There is no room here for making personal petitions.

_____

_____

_____

_____

PURE HEART – ASK HIM TO PURIFY YOUR MIND AND HEART: Replace negative thoughts with higher thoughts. God's thoughts are noble, pure, lovely, excellent, right, true, and admirable. Ask God to reveal areas in your life that grieve the Holy Spirit. Confess with a contrite heart and receive forgiveness. As you confess, turn your palms up and release your sin, worry, and anxiety over to God. Now turn your palms down and receive God's love, mercy, favor, and grace.

_____

_____

_____

THANKFULNESS – NAME THOSE THINGS YOU ARE THANKFUL FOR: There's always something to be grateful for. Name them one by one and come back often to rekindle the joy of each one of them.

O

O

O

O

O

O

O

	TASKS
REFLECTION & REVELATION – PRACTICE LISTENING FOR GOD: God promises that if you draw near to Him, He will tell you things you do not know. Who does God bring to mind? Where is God leading you? Reflect on God's perspective.	
PRAYER – YOU HAVE NOT BECAUSE YOU ASK NOT: Pray for family, friends, relationships, unity, community, world, church, favor, wisdom, God's will, work, and your future. Pray about anything and everything, without ceasing.	
OBEDIENCE – STAND, SHARE, SERVE: Take steps of faith, and obey promptly. The level of miracles in your life will be directly related to your level of obedience. Faith without works is dead. You have an assignment, a destiny to fulfill.	
	6 am
	7 am
	8 am
	9 am
	10 am
	11 am
	12 pm
	1 pm
	2 pm
	3 pm
	4 pm
	5 pm
	6 pm
	7 pm
	8 pm
	9 pm

Date:

SCRIPTURE – DRAW CLOSER TO THE KING OF KINGS: Use your name in the place of a character in the scripture you're reading; imagine yourself in that time, using all 5 senses. Pray scripture back to God. Write the scripture down, read it, repeat it out loud throughout the day, memorize it, and meditate on it.

_____

_____

_____

_____

_____

_____

_____

_____

_____

_____

_____

_____

_____

_____

WORSHIP – PRAISE HIM FOR WHO HE IS: How will you glorify and magnify Him today? There is no room here for making personal petitions.

_____

_____

_____

PURE HEART – ASK HIM TO PURIFY YOUR MIND AND HEART: Replace negative thoughts with higher thoughts. God's thoughts are noble, pure, lovely, excellent, right, true, and admirable. Ask God to reveal areas in your life that grieve the Holy Spirit. Confess with a contrite heart and receive forgiveness. As you confess, turn your palms up and release your sin, worry, and anxiety over to God. Now turn your palms down and receive God's love, mercy, favor, and grace.

_____

_____

_____

THANKFULNESS – NAME THOSE THINGS YOU ARE THANKFUL FOR: There's always something to be grateful for. Name them one by one and come back often to rekindle the joy of each one of them.

O

O

O

O

O

O

O

REFLECTION & REVELATION – PRACTICE LISTENING FOR GOD: God promises that if you draw near to Him, He will tell you things you do not know. Who does God bring to mind? Where is God leading you? Reflect on God's perspective.	TASKS
PRAYER – YOU HAVE NOT BECAUSE YOU ASK NOT: Pray for family, friends, relationships, unity, community, world, church, favor, wisdom, God's will, work, and your future. Pray about anything and everything, without ceasing.	
OBEDIENCE – STAND, SHARE, SERVE: Take steps of faith, and obey promptly. The level of miracles in your life will be directly related to your level of obedience. Faith without works is dead. You have an assignment, a destiny to fulfill.	
	6 am
	7 am
	8 am
	9 am
	10 am
	11 am
	12 pm
	1 pm
	2 pm
	3 pm
	4 pm
	5 pm
	6 pm
	7 pm
	8 pm
	9 pm

Date:

SCRIPTURE – DRAW CLOSER TO THE KING OF KINGS: Use your name in the place of a character in the scripture you're reading; imagine yourself in that time, using all 5 senses. Pray scripture back to God. Write the scripture down, read it, repeat it out loud throughout the day, memorize it, and meditate on it.

WORSHIP – PRAISE HIM FOR WHO HE IS: How will you glorify and magnify Him today? There is no room here for making personal petitions.

PURE HEART – ASK HIM TO PURIFY YOUR MIND AND HEART: Replace negative thoughts with higher thoughts. God's thoughts are noble, pure, lovely, excellent, right, true, and admirable. Ask God to reveal areas in your life that grieve the Holy Spirit. Confess with a contrite heart and receive forgiveness. As you confess, turn your palms up and release your sin, worry, and anxiety over to God. Now turn your palms down and receive God's love, mercy, favor, and grace.

THANKFULNESS – NAME THOSE THINGS YOU ARE THANKFUL FOR: There's always something to be grateful for. Name them one by one and come back often to rekindle the joy of each one of them.

O

O

O

O

O

O

O

REFLECTION & REVELATION – PRACTICE LISTENING FOR GOD: God promises that if you draw near to Him, He will tell you things you do not know. Who does God bring to mind? Where is God leading you? Reflect on God's perspective.	TASKS
PRAYER – YOU HAVE NOT BECAUSE YOU ASK NOT: Pray for family, friends, relationships, unity, community, world, church, favor, wisdom, God's will, work, and your future. Pray about anything and everything, without ceasing.	
OBEDIENCE – STAND, SHARE, SERVE: Take steps of faith, and obey promptly. The level of miracles in your life will be directly related to your level of obedience. Faith without works is dead. You have an assignment, a destiny to fulfill.	
	6 am
	7 am
	8 am
	9 am
	10 am
	11 am
	12 pm
	1 pm
	2 pm
	3 pm
	4 pm
	5 pm
	6 pm
	7 pm
	8 pm
	9 pm

Date:

SCRIPTURE – DRAW CLOSER TO THE KING OF KINGS: Use your name in the place of a character in the scripture you're reading; imagine yourself in that time, using all 5 senses. Pray scripture back to God. Write the scripture down, read it, repeat it out loud throughout the day, memorize it, and meditate on it.

_____
_____
_____
_____
_____
_____
_____
_____
_____
_____
_____
_____

WORSHIP – PRAISE HIM FOR WHO HE IS: How will you glorify and magnify Him today? There is no room here for making personal petitions.

_____
_____
_____
_____

PURE HEART – ASK HIM TO PURIFY YOUR MIND AND HEART: Replace negative thoughts with higher thoughts. God's thoughts are noble, pure, lovely, excellent, right, true, and admirable. Ask God to reveal areas in your life that grieve the Holy Spirit. Confess with a contrite heart and receive forgiveness. As you confess, turn your palms up and release your sin, worry, and anxiety over to God. Now turn your palms down and receive God's love, mercy, favor, and grace.

_____
_____
_____

THANKFULNESS – NAME THOSE THINGS YOU ARE THANKFUL FOR: There's always something to be grateful for. Name them one by one and come back often to rekindle the joy of each one of them.

O _____

O _____

O _____

O _____

O _____

O _____

O _____

REFLECTION & REVELATION – PRACTICE LISTENING FOR GOD: God promises that if you draw near to Him, He will tell you things you do not know. Who does God bring to mind? Where is God leading you? Reflect on God's perspective.	TASKS
PRAYER – YOU HAVE NOT BECAUSE YOU ASK NOT: Pray for family, friends, relationships, unity, community, world, church, favor, wisdom, God's will, work, and your future. Pray about anything and everything, without ceasing.	
OBEDIENCE – STAND, SHARE, SERVE: Take steps of faith, and obey promptly. The level of miracles in your life will be directly related to your level of obedience. Faith without works is dead. You have an assignment, a destiny to fulfill.	
	6 am
	7 am
	8 am
	9 am
	10 am
	11 am
	12 pm
	1 pm
	2 pm
	3 pm
	4 pm
	5 pm
	6 pm
	7 pm
	8 pm
	9 pm

Date:

SCRIPTURE – DRAW CLOSER TO THE KING OF KINGS: Use your name in the place of a character in the scripture you're reading; imagine yourself in that time, using all 5 senses. Pray scripture back to God. Write the scripture down, read it, repeat it out loud throughout the day, memorize it, and meditate on it.

_____

_____

_____

_____

_____

_____

_____

_____

_____

_____

_____

_____

_____

WORSHIP – PRAISE HIM FOR WHO HE IS: How will you glorify and magnify Him today? There is no room here for making personal petitions.

_____

_____

_____

_____

PURE HEART – ASK HIM TO PURIFY YOUR MIND AND HEART: Replace negative thoughts with higher thoughts. God's thoughts are noble, pure, lovely, excellent, right, true, and admirable. Ask God to reveal areas in your life that grieve the Holy Spirit. Confess with a contrite heart and receive forgiveness. As you confess, turn your palms up and release your sin, worry, and anxiety over to God. Now turn your palms down and receive God's love, mercy, favor, and grace.

_____

_____

_____

THANKFULNESS – NAME THOSE THINGS YOU ARE THANKFUL FOR: There's always something to be grateful for. Name them one by one and come back often to rekindle the joy of each one of them.

O

O

O

O

O

O

O

REFLECTION & REVELATION – PRACTICE LISTENING FOR GOD: God promises that if you draw near to Him, He will tell you things you do not know. Who does God bring to mind? Where is God leading you? Reflect on God's perspective.	TASKS
PRAYER – YOU HAVE NOT BECAUSE YOU ASK NOT: Pray for family, friends, relationships, unity, community, world, church, favor, wisdom, God's will, work, and your future. Pray about anything and everything, without ceasing.	
OBEDIENCE – STAND, SHARE, SERVE: Take steps of faith, and obey promptly. The level of miracles in your life will be directly related to your level of obedience. Faith without works is dead. You have an assignment, a destiny to fulfill.	
	6 am
	7 am
	8 am
	9 am
	10 am
	11 am
	12 pm
	1 pm
	2 pm
	3 pm
	4 pm
	5 pm
	6 pm
	7 pm
	8 pm
	9 pm

WEEKLY FOCUS

Last Week's Reflection
Areas to Celebrate:
Areas to Improve:
What did I learn

This Week's Planning
Plan for joyful occasions. Joy is your strength, refreshment, energy, and beauty. What are you looking forward to this week? Find something to laugh about and share it.
Projects/Areas of focus this week:

- [ ]
- [ ]
- [ ]
- [ ]
- [ ]
- [ ]

AREAS TO SIMPLIFY – where to set godly boundaries

	What is important	What is not important	Why	What are Facts/Feelings	Benefits of continuing/not continuing	Pray about possibilities and solutions
Time						
Energy						
Money						
Relationships						
Possessions						

FASTING: Take authority over what controls me; lean on God; keep Christ-focused
What to fast:
Time to fast:
How to fast:
Check motives:

ADDITIONAL REFLECTION

Date:

SCRIPTURE – DRAW CLOSER TO THE KING OF KINGS: Use your name in the place of a character in the scripture you're reading; imagine yourself in that time, using all 5 senses. Pray scripture back to God. Write the scripture down, read it, repeat it out loud throughout the day, memorize it, and meditate on it.

WORSHIP – PRAISE HIM FOR WHO HE IS: How will you glorify and magnify Him today? There is no room here for making personal petitions.

PURE HEART – ASK HIM TO PURIFY YOUR MIND AND HEART: Replace negative thoughts with higher thoughts. God's thoughts are noble, pure, lovely, excellent, right, true, and admirable. Ask God to reveal areas in your life that grieve the Holy Spirit. Confess with a contrite heart and receive forgiveness. As you confess, turn your palms up and release your sin, worry, and anxiety over to God. Now turn your palms down and receive God's love, mercy, favor, and grace.

THANKFULNESS – NAME THOSE THINGS YOU ARE THANKFUL FOR: There's always something to be grateful for. Name them one by one and come back often to rekindle the joy of each one of them.

O

O

O

O

O

O

O

REFLECTION & REVELATION – PRACTICE LISTENING FOR GOD: God promises that if you draw near to Him, He will tell you things you do not know. Who does God bring to mind? Where is God leading you? Reflect on God's perspective.	TASKS
PRAYER – YOU HAVE NOT BECAUSE YOU ASK NOT: Pray for family, friends, relationships, unity, community, world, church, favor, wisdom, God's will, work, and your future. Pray about anything and everything, without ceasing.	
OBEDIENCE – STAND, SHARE, SERVE: Take steps of faith, and obey promptly. The level of miracles in your life will be directly related to your level of obedience. Faith without works is dead. You have an assignment, a destiny to fulfill.	
	6 am
	7 am
	8 am
	9 am
	10 am
	11 am
	12 pm
	1 pm
	2 pm
	3 pm
	4 pm
	5 pm
	6 pm
	7 pm
	8 pm
	9 pm

Date:

SCRIPTURE – DRAW CLOSER TO THE KING OF KINGS: Use your name in the place of a character in the scripture you're reading; imagine yourself in that time, using all 5 senses. Pray scripture back to God. Write the scripture down, read it, repeat it out loud throughout the day, memorize it, and meditate on it.

WORSHIP – PRAISE HIM FOR WHO HE IS: How will you glorify and magnify Him today? There is no room here for making personal petitions.

PURE HEART – ASK HIM TO PURIFY YOUR MIND AND HEART: Replace negative thoughts with higher thoughts. God's thoughts are noble, pure, lovely, excellent, right, true, and admirable. Ask God to reveal areas in your life that grieve the Holy Spirit. Confess with a contrite heart and receive forgiveness. As you confess, turn your palms up and release your sin, worry, and anxiety over to God. Now turn your palms down and receive God's love, mercy, favor, and grace.

THANKFULNESS – NAME THOSE THINGS YOU ARE THANKFUL FOR: There's always something to be grateful for. Name them one by one and come back often to rekindle the joy of each one of them.

O

O

O

O

O

O

O

	TASKS
REFLECTION & REVELATION – PRACTICE LISTENING FOR GOD: God promises that if you draw near to Him, He will tell you things you do not know. Who does God bring to mind? Where is God leading you? Reflect on God's perspective.	
PRAYER – YOU HAVE NOT BECAUSE YOU ASK NOT: Pray for family, friends, relationships, unity, community, world, church, favor, wisdom, God's will, work, and your future. Pray about anything and everything, without ceasing.	
OBEDIENCE – STAND, SHARE, SERVE: Take steps of faith, and obey promptly. The level of miracles in your life will be directly related to your level of obedience. Faith without works is dead. You have an assignment, a destiny to fulfill.	
	6 am
	7 am
	8 am
	9 am
	10 am
	11 am
	12 pm
	1 pm
	2 pm
	3 pm
	4 pm
	5 pm
	6 pm
	7 pm
	8 pm
	9 pm

Date:

SCRIPTURE – DRAW CLOSER TO THE KING OF KINGS: Use your name in the place of a character in the scripture you're reading; imagine yourself in that time, using all 5 senses. Pray scripture back to God. Write the scripture down, read it, repeat it out loud throughout the day, memorize it, and meditate on it.

_____
_____
_____
_____
_____
_____
_____
_____
_____
_____
_____
_____

WORSHIP – PRAISE HIM FOR WHO HE IS: How will you glorify and magnify Him today? There is no room here for making personal petitions.

_____
_____
_____

PURE HEART – ASK HIM TO PURIFY YOUR MIND AND HEART: Replace negative thoughts with higher thoughts. God's thoughts are noble, pure, lovely, excellent, right, true, and admirable. Ask God to reveal areas in your life that grieve the Holy Spirit. Confess with a contrite heart and receive forgiveness. As you confess, turn your palms up and release your sin, worry, and anxiety over to God. Now turn your palms down and receive God's love, mercy, favor, and grace.

_____
_____
_____

THANKFULNESS – NAME THOSE THINGS YOU ARE THANKFUL FOR: There's always something to be grateful for. Name them one by one and come back often to rekindle the joy of each one of them.

O
O
O
O
O
O
O

REFLECTION & REVELATION – PRACTICE LISTENING FOR GOD: God promises that if you draw near to Him, He will tell you things you do not know. Who does God bring to mind? Where is God leading you? Reflect on God's perspective.	TASKS
PRAYER – YOU HAVE NOT BECAUSE YOU ASK NOT: Pray for family, friends, relationships, unity, community, world, church, favor, wisdom, God's will, work, and your future. Pray about anything and everything, without ceasing.	
OBEDIENCE – STAND, SHARE, SERVE: Take steps of faith, and obey promptly. The level of miracles in your life will be directly related to your level of obedience. Faith without works is dead. You have an assignment, a destiny to fulfill.	
	6 am
	7 am
	8 am
	9 am
	10 am
	11 am
	12 pm
	1 pm
	2 pm
	3 pm
	4 pm
	5 pm
	6 pm
	7 pm
	8 pm
	9 pm

Date:

SCRIPTURE – DRAW CLOSER TO THE KING OF KINGS: Use your name in the place of a character in the scripture you're reading; imagine yourself in that time, using all 5 senses. Pray scripture back to God. Write the scripture down, read it, repeat it out loud throughout the day, memorize it, and meditate on it.

_____
_____
_____
_____
_____
_____
_____
_____
_____
_____
_____
_____
_____
_____
_____

WORSHIP – PRAISE HIM FOR WHO HE IS: How will you glorify and magnify Him today? There is no room here for making personal petitions.

_____
_____
_____
_____

PURE HEART – ASK HIM TO PURIFY YOUR MIND AND HEART: Replace negative thoughts with higher thoughts. God's thoughts are noble, pure, lovely, excellent, right, true, and admirable. Ask God to reveal areas in your life that grieve the Holy Spirit. Confess with a contrite heart and receive forgiveness. As you confess, turn your palms up and release your sin, worry, and anxiety over to God. Now turn your palms down and receive God's love, mercy, favor, and grace.

_____
_____
_____

THANKFULNESS – NAME THOSE THINGS YOU ARE THANKFUL FOR: There's always something to be grateful for. Name them one by one and come back often to rekindle the joy of each one of them.

O _____

O _____

O _____

O _____

O _____

O _____

O _____

REFLECTION & REVELATION – PRACTICE LISTENING FOR GOD: God promises that if you draw near to Him, He will tell you things you do not know. Who does God bring to mind? Where is God leading you? Reflect on God's perspective.	TASKS
PRAYER – YOU HAVE NOT BECAUSE YOU ASK NOT: Pray for family, friends, relationships, unity, community, world, church, favor, wisdom, God's will, work, and your future. Pray about anything and everything, without ceasing.	
OBEDIENCE – STAND, SHARE, SERVE: Take steps of faith, and obey promptly. The level of miracles in your life will be directly related to your level of obedience. Faith without works is dead. You have an assignment, a destiny to fulfill.	
	6 am
	7 am
	8 am
	9 am
	10 am
	11 am
	12 pm
	1 pm
	2 pm
	3 pm
	4 pm
	5 pm
	6 pm
	7 pm
	8 pm
	9 pm

Date:

SCRIPTURE – DRAW CLOSER TO THE KING OF KINGS: Use your name in the place of a character in the scripture you're reading; imagine yourself in that time, using all 5 senses. Pray scripture back to God. Write the scripture down, read it, repeat it out loud throughout the day, memorize it, and meditate on it.

_____
_____
_____
_____
_____
_____
_____
_____
_____
_____
_____
_____
_____

WORSHIP – PRAISE HIM FOR WHO HE IS: How will you glorify and magnify Him today? There is no room here for making personal petitions.

_____
_____
_____

PURE HEART – ASK HIM TO PURIFY YOUR MIND AND HEART: Replace negative thoughts with higher thoughts. God's thoughts are noble, pure, lovely, excellent, right, true, and admirable. Ask God to reveal areas in your life that grieve the Holy Spirit. Confess with a contrite heart and receive forgiveness. As you confess, turn your palms up and release your sin, worry, and anxiety over to God. Now turn your palms down and receive God's love, mercy, favor, and grace.

_____
_____
_____

THANKFULNESS – NAME THOSE THINGS YOU ARE THANKFUL FOR: There's always something to be grateful for. Name them one by one and come back often to rekindle the joy of each one of them.

O
O
O
O
O
O
O

REFLECTION & REVELATION – PRACTICE LISTENING FOR GOD: God promises that if you draw near to Him, He will tell you things you do not know. Who does God bring to mind? Where is God leading you? Reflect on God's perspective.	TASKS
PRAYER – YOU HAVE NOT BECAUSE YOU ASK NOT: Pray for family, friends, relationships, unity, community, world, church, favor, wisdom, God's will, work, and your future. Pray about anything and everything, without ceasing.	
OBEDIENCE – STAND, SHARE, SERVE: Take steps of faith, and obey promptly. The level of miracles in your life will be directly related to your level of obedience. Faith without works is dead. You have an assignment, a destiny to fulfill.	
	6 am
	7 am
	8 am
	9 am
	10 am
	11 am
	12 pm
	1 pm
	2 pm
	3 pm
	4 pm
	5 pm
	6 pm
	7 pm
	8 pm
	9 pm

Date:

SCRIPTURE – DRAW CLOSER TO THE KING OF KINGS: Use your name in the place of a character in the scripture you're reading; imagine yourself in that time, using all 5 senses. Pray scripture back to God. Write the scripture down, read it, repeat it out loud throughout the day, memorize it, and meditate on it.

_____
_____
_____
_____
_____
_____
_____
_____
_____
_____
_____
_____

WORSHIP – PRAISE HIM FOR WHO HE IS: How will you glorify and magnify Him today? There is no room here for making personal petitions.

_____
_____
_____
_____

PURE HEART – ASK HIM TO PURIFY YOUR MIND AND HEART: Replace negative thoughts with higher thoughts. God's thoughts are noble, pure, lovely, excellent, right, true, and admirable. Ask God to reveal areas in your life that grieve the Holy Spirit. Confess with a contrite heart and receive forgiveness. As you confess, turn your palms up and release your sin, worry, and anxiety over to God. Now turn your palms down and receive God's love, mercy, favor, and grace.

_____
_____
_____

THANKFULNESS – NAME THOSE THINGS YOU ARE THANKFUL FOR: There's always something to be grateful for. Name them one by one and come back often to rekindle the joy of each one of them.

O
O
O
O
O
O
O

REFLECTION & REVELATION – PRACTICE LISTENING FOR GOD: God promises that if you draw near to Him, He will tell you things you do not know. Who does God bring to mind? Where is God leading you? Reflect on God's perspective.	TASKS
PRAYER – YOU HAVE NOT BECAUSE YOU ASK NOT: Pray for family, friends, relationships, unity, community, world, church, favor, wisdom, God's will, work, and your future. Pray about anything and everything, without ceasing.	
OBEDIENCE – STAND, SHARE, SERVE: Take steps of faith, and obey promptly. The level of miracles in your life will be directly related to your level of obedience. Faith without works is dead. You have an assignment, a destiny to fulfill.	
	6 am
	7 am
	8 am
	9 am
	10 am
	11 am
	12 pm
	1 pm
	2 pm
	3 pm
	4 pm
	5 pm
	6 pm
	7 pm
	8 pm
	9 pm

Date:

SCRIPTURE – DRAW CLOSER TO THE KING OF KINGS: Use your name in the place of a character in the scripture you're reading; imagine yourself in that time, using all 5 senses. Pray scripture back to God. Write the scripture down, read it, repeat it out loud throughout the day, memorize it, and meditate on it.

_____
_____
_____
_____
_____
_____
_____
_____
_____
_____
_____
_____

WORSHIP – PRAISE HIM FOR WHO HE IS: How will you glorify and magnify Him today? There is no room here for making personal petitions.

_____
_____
_____
_____

PURE HEART – ASK HIM TO PURIFY YOUR MIND AND HEART: Replace negative thoughts with higher thoughts. God's thoughts are noble, pure, lovely, excellent, right, true, and admirable. Ask God to reveal areas in your life that grieve the Holy Spirit. Confess with a contrite heart and receive forgiveness. As you confess, turn your palms up and release your sin, worry, and anxiety over to God. Now turn your palms down and receive God's love, mercy, favor, and grace.

_____
_____
_____

THANKFULNESS – NAME THOSE THINGS YOU ARE THANKFUL FOR: There's always something to be grateful for. Name them one by one and come back often to rekindle the joy of each one of them.

O
O
O
O
O
O
O

REFLECTION & REVELATION – PRACTICE LISTENING FOR GOD: God promises that if you draw near to Him, He will tell you things you do not know. Who does God bring to mind? Where is God leading you? Reflect on God's perspective.	TASKS
PRAYER – YOU HAVE NOT BECAUSE YOU ASK NOT: Pray for family, friends, relationships, unity, community, world, church, favor, wisdom, God's will, work, and your future. Pray about anything and everything, without ceasing.	
OBEDIENCE – STAND, SHARE, SERVE: Take steps of faith, and obey promptly. The level of miracles in your life will be directly related to your level of obedience. Faith without works is dead. You have an assignment, a destiny to fulfill.	
	6 am
	7 am
	8 am
	9 am
	10 am
	11 am
	12 pm
	1 pm
	2 pm
	3 pm
	4 pm
	5 pm
	6 pm
	7 pm
	8 pm
	9 pm

WEEKLY FOCUS

Last Week's Reflection
Areas to Celebrate:
Areas to Improve:
What did I learn

This Week's Planning
Plan for joyful occasions. Joy is your strength, refreshment, energy, and beauty. What are you looking forward to this week? Find something to laugh about and share it.
Projects/Areas of focus this week:
☐
☐
☐
☐
☐
☐
☐

AREAS TO SIMPLIFY – where to set godly boundaries

	What is important	What is not important	Why	What are Facts/Feelings	Benefits of continuing/not continuing	Pray about possibilities and solutions
Time						
Energy						
Money						
Relationships						
Possessions						

FASTING: Take authority over what controls me; lean on God; keep Christ-focused
What to fast:
Time to fast:
How to fast:
Check motives:

ADDITIONAL REFLECTION

Date:

SCRIPTURE – DRAW CLOSER TO THE KING OF KINGS: Use your name in the place of a character in the scripture you're reading; imagine yourself in that time, using all 5 senses. Pray scripture back to God. Write the scripture down, read it, repeat it out loud throughout the day, memorize it, and meditate on it.

WORSHIP – PRAISE HIM FOR WHO HE IS: How will you glorify and magnify Him today? There is no room here for making personal petitions.

PURE HEART – ASK HIM TO PURIFY YOUR MIND AND HEART: Replace negative thoughts with higher thoughts. God's thoughts are noble, pure, lovely, excellent, right, true, and admirable. Ask God to reveal areas in your life that grieve the Holy Spirit. Confess with a contrite heart and receive forgiveness. As you confess, turn your palms up and release your sin, worry, and anxiety over to God. Now turn your palms down and receive God's love, mercy, favor, and grace.

THANKFULNESS – NAME THOSE THINGS YOU ARE THANKFUL FOR: There's always something to be grateful for. Name them one by one and come back often to rekindle the joy of each one of them.

O

O

O

O

O

O

O

	TASKS
REFLECTION & REVELATION – PRACTICE LISTENING FOR GOD: God promises that if you draw near to Him, He will tell you things you do not know. Who does God bring to mind? Where is God leading you? Reflect on God's perspective.	
PRAYER – YOU HAVE NOT BECAUSE YOU ASK NOT: Pray for family, friends, relationships, unity, community, world, church, favor, wisdom, God's will, work, and your future. Pray about anything and everything, without ceasing.	
OBEDIENCE – STAND, SHARE, SERVE: Take steps of faith, and obey promptly. The level of miracles in your life will be directly related to your level of obedience. Faith without works is dead. You have an assignment, a destiny to fulfill.	
	6 am
	7 am
	8 am
	9 am
	10 am
	11 am
	12 pm
	1 pm
	2 pm
	3 pm
	4 pm
	5 pm
	6 pm
	7 pm
	8 pm
	9 pm

Date:

SCRIPTURE – DRAW CLOSER TO THE KING OF KINGS: Use your name in the place of a character in the scripture you're reading; imagine yourself in that time, using all 5 senses. Pray scripture back to God. Write the scripture down, read it, repeat it out loud throughout the day, memorize it, and meditate on it.

WORSHIP – PRAISE HIM FOR WHO HE IS: How will you glorify and magnify Him today? There is no room here for making personal petitions.

PURE HEART – ASK HIM TO PURIFY YOUR MIND AND HEART: Replace negative thoughts with higher thoughts. God's thoughts are noble, pure, lovely, excellent, right, true, and admirable. Ask God to reveal areas in your life that grieve the Holy Spirit. Confess with a contrite heart and receive forgiveness. As you confess, turn your palms up and release your sin, worry, and anxiety over to God. Now turn your palms down and receive God's love, mercy, favor, and grace.

THANKFULNESS – NAME THOSE THINGS YOU ARE THANKFUL FOR: There's always something to be grateful for. Name them one by one and come back often to rekindle the joy of each one of them.

O

O

O

O

O

O

O

REFLECTION & REVELATION – PRACTICE LISTENING FOR GOD: God promises that if you draw near to Him, He will tell you things you do not know. Who does God bring to mind? Where is God leading you? Reflect on God's perspective.	TASKS
PRAYER – YOU HAVE NOT BECAUSE YOU ASK NOT: Pray for family, friends, relationships, unity, community, world, church, favor, wisdom, God's will, work, and your future. Pray about anything and everything, without ceasing.	
OBEDIENCE – STAND, SHARE, SERVE: Take steps of faith, and obey promptly. The level of miracles in your life will be directly related to your level of obedience. Faith without works is dead. You have an assignment, a destiny to fulfill.	
	6 am
	7 am
	8 am
	9 am
	10 am
	11 am
	12 pm
	1 pm
	2 pm
	3 pm
	4 pm
	5 pm
	6 pm
	7 pm
	8 pm
	9 pm

Date:

SCRIPTURE – DRAW CLOSER TO THE KING OF KINGS: Use your name in the place of a character in the scripture you're reading; imagine yourself in that time, using all 5 senses. Pray scripture back to God. Write the scripture down, read it, repeat it out loud throughout the day, memorize it, and meditate on it.

WORSHIP – PRAISE HIM FOR WHO HE IS: How will you glorify and magnify Him today? There is no room here for making personal petitions.

PURE HEART – ASK HIM TO PURIFY YOUR MIND AND HEART: Replace negative thoughts with higher thoughts. God's thoughts are noble, pure, lovely, excellent, right, true, and admirable. Ask God to reveal areas in your life that grieve the Holy Spirit. Confess with a contrite heart and receive forgiveness. As you confess, turn your palms up and release your sin, worry, and anxiety over to God. Now turn your palms down and receive God's love, mercy, favor, and grace.

THANKFULNESS – NAME THOSE THINGS YOU ARE THANKFUL FOR: There's always something to be grateful for. Name them one by one and come back often to rekindle the joy of each one of them.

O

O

O'

O

O

O

O

REFLECTION & REVELATION – PRACTICE LISTENING FOR GOD: God promises that if you draw near to Him, He will tell you things you do not know. Who does God bring to mind? Where is God leading you? Reflect on God's perspective.	TASKS
PRAYER – YOU HAVE NOT BECAUSE YOU ASK NOT: Pray for family, friends, relationships, unity, community, world, church, favor, wisdom, God's will, work, and your future. Pray about anything and everything, without ceasing.	
OBEDIENCE – STAND, SHARE, SERVE: Take steps of faith, and obey promptly. The level of miracles in your life will be directly related to your level of obedience. Faith without works is dead. You have an assignment, a destiny to fulfill.	
	6 am
	7 am
	8 am
	9 am
	10 am
	11 am
	12 pm
	1 pm
	2 pm
	3 pm
	4 pm
	5 pm
	6 pm
	7 pm
	8 pm
	9 pm

Date:

SCRIPTURE – DRAW CLOSER TO THE KING OF KINGS: Use your name in the place of a character in the scripture you're reading; imagine yourself in that time, using all 5 senses. Pray scripture back to God. Write the scripture down, read it, repeat it out loud throughout the day, memorize it, and meditate on it.

WORSHIP – PRAISE HIM FOR WHO HE IS: How will you glorify and magnify Him today? There is no room here for making personal petitions.

PURE HEART – ASK HIM TO PURIFY YOUR MIND AND HEART: Replace negative thoughts with higher thoughts. God's thoughts are noble, pure, lovely, excellent, right, true, and admirable. Ask God to reveal areas in your life that grieve the Holy Spirit. Confess with a contrite heart and receive forgiveness. As you confess, turn your palms up and release your sin, worry, and anxiety over to God. Now turn your palms down and receive God's love, mercy, favor, and grace.

THANKFULNESS – NAME THOSE THINGS YOU ARE THANKFUL FOR: There's always something to be grateful for. Name them one by one and come back often to rekindle the joy of each one of them.

O

O

O

O

O

O

O

REFLECTION & REVELATION – PRACTICE LISTENING FOR GOD: God promises that if you draw near to Him, He will tell you things you do not know. Who does God bring to mind? Where is God leading you? Reflect on God's perspective.	TASKS
PRAYER – YOU HAVE NOT BECAUSE YOU ASK NOT: Pray for family, friends, relationships, unity, community, world, church, favor, wisdom, God's will, work, and your future. Pray about anything and everything, without ceasing.	
OBEDIENCE – STAND, SHARE, SERVE: Take steps of faith, and obey promptly. The level of miracles in your life will be directly related to your level of obedience. Faith without works is dead. You have an assignment, a destiny to fulfill.	
	6 am
	7 am
	8 am
	9 am
	10 am
	11 am
	12 pm
	1 pm
	2 pm
	3 pm
	4 pm
	5 pm
	6 pm
	7 pm
	8 pm
	9 pm

Date:

SCRIPTURE – DRAW CLOSER TO THE KING OF KINGS: Use your name in the place of a character in the scripture you're reading; imagine yourself in that time, using all 5 senses. Pray scripture back to God. Write the scripture down, read it, repeat it out loud throughout the day, memorize it, and meditate on it.

_____
_____
_____
_____
_____
_____
_____
_____
_____
_____
_____
_____

WORSHIP – PRAISE HIM FOR WHO HE IS: How will you glorify and magnify Him today? There is no room here for making personal petitions.

_____
_____
_____
_____

PURE HEART – ASK HIM TO PURIFY YOUR MIND AND HEART: Replace negative thoughts with higher thoughts. God's thoughts are noble, pure, lovely, excellent, right, true, and admirable. Ask God to reveal areas in your life that grieve the Holy Spirit. Confess with a contrite heart and receive forgiveness. As you confess, turn your palms up and release your sin, worry, and anxiety over to God. Now turn your palms down and receive God's love, mercy, favor, and grace.

_____
_____
_____

THANKFULNESS – NAME THOSE THINGS YOU ARE THANKFUL FOR: There's always something to be grateful for. Name them one by one and come back often to rekindle the joy of each one of them.

O _____

O _____

O _____

O _____

O _____

O _____

O _____

REFLECTION & REVELATION – PRACTICE LISTENING FOR GOD: God promises that if you draw near to Him, He will tell you things you do not know. Who does God bring to mind? Where is God leading you? Reflect on God's perspective.	TASKS
PRAYER – YOU HAVE NOT BECAUSE YOU ASK NOT: Pray for family, friends, relationships, unity, community, world, church, favor, wisdom, God's will, work, and your future. Pray about anything and everything, without ceasing.	
OBEDIENCE – STAND, SHARE, SERVE: Take steps of faith, and obey promptly. The level of miracles in your life will be directly related to your level of obedience. Faith without works is dead. You have an assignment, a destiny to fulfill.	
	6 am
	7 am
	8 am
	9 am
	10 am
	11 am
	12 pm
	1 pm
	2 pm
	3 pm
	4 pm
	5 pm
	6 pm
	7 pm
	8 pm
	9 pm

Date:

SCRIPTURE – DRAW CLOSER TO THE KING OF KINGS: Use your name in the place of a character in the scripture you're reading; imagine yourself in that time, using all 5 senses. Pray scripture back to God. Write the scripture down, read it, repeat it out loud throughout the day, memorize it, and meditate on it.

_____

_____

_____

_____

_____

_____

_____

_____

_____

_____

_____

_____

WORSHIP – PRAISE HIM FOR WHO HE IS: How will you glorify and magnify Him today? There is no room here for making personal petitions.

_____

_____

_____

PURE HEART – ASK HIM TO PURIFY YOUR MIND AND HEART: Replace negative thoughts with higher thoughts. God's thoughts are noble, pure, lovely, excellent, right, true, and admirable. Ask God to reveal areas in your life that grieve the Holy Spirit. Confess with a contrite heart and receive forgiveness. As you confess, turn your palms up and release your sin, worry, and anxiety over to God. Now turn your palms down and receive God's love, mercy, favor, and grace.

_____

_____

_____

THANKFULNESS – NAME THOSE THINGS YOU ARE THANKFUL FOR: There's always something to be grateful for. Name them one by one and come back often to rekindle the joy of each one of them.

O

O

O

O

O

O

O

REFLECTION & REVELATION – PRACTICE LISTENING FOR GOD: God promises that if you draw near to Him, He will tell you things you do not know. Who does God bring to mind? Where is God leading you? Reflect on God's perspective.	TASKS
PRAYER – YOU HAVE NOT BECAUSE YOU ASK NOT: Pray for family, friends, relationships, unity, community, world, church, favor, wisdom, God's will, work, and your future. Pray about anything and everything, without ceasing.	
OBEDIENCE – STAND, SHARE, SERVE: Take steps of faith, and obey promptly. The level of miracles in your life will be directly related to your level of obedience. Faith without works is dead. You have an assignment, a destiny to fulfill.	
	6 am
	7 am
	8 am
	9 am
	10 am
	11 am
	12 pm
	1 pm
	2 pm
	3 pm
	4 pm
	5 pm
	6 pm
	7 pm
	8 pm
	9 pm

Date:

SCRIPTURE – DRAW CLOSER TO THE KING OF KINGS: Use your name in the place of a character in the scripture you're reading; imagine yourself in that time, using all 5 senses. Pray scripture back to God. Write the scripture down, read it, repeat it out loud throughout the day, memorize it, and meditate on it.

_____
_____
_____
_____
_____
_____
_____
_____
_____
_____
_____
_____
_____

WORSHIP – PRAISE HIM FOR WHO HE IS: How will you glorify and magnify Him today? There is no room here for making personal petitions.

_____
_____
_____
_____

PURE HEART – ASK HIM TO PURIFY YOUR MIND AND HEART: Replace negative thoughts with higher thoughts. God's thoughts are noble, pure, lovely, excellent, right, true, and admirable. Ask God to reveal areas in your life that grieve the Holy Spirit. Confess with a contrite heart and receive forgiveness. As you confess, turn your palms up and release your sin, worry, and anxiety over to God. Now turn your palms down and receive God's love, mercy, favor, and grace.

_____
_____
_____

THANKFULNESS – NAME THOSE THINGS YOU ARE THANKFUL FOR: There's always something to be grateful for. Name them one by one and come back often to rekindle the joy of each one of them.

O

O

O

O

O

O

O

	TASKS
REFLECTION & REVELATION – PRACTICE LISTENING FOR GOD: God promises that if you draw near to Him, He will tell you things you do not know. Who does God bring to mind? Where is God leading you? Reflect on God's perspective.	
PRAYER – YOU HAVE NOT BECAUSE YOU ASK NOT: Pray for family, friends, relationships, unity, community, world, church, favor, wisdom, God's will, work, and your future. Pray about anything and everything, without ceasing.	
OBEDIENCE – STAND, SHARE, SERVE: Take steps of faith, and obey promptly. The level of miracles in your life will be directly related to your level of obedience. Faith without works is dead. You have an assignment, a destiny to fulfill.	
	6 am
	7 am
	8 am
	9 am
	10 am
	11 am
	12 pm
	1 pm
	2 pm
	3 pm
	4 pm
	5 pm
	6 pm
	7 pm
	8 pm
	9 pm

Last Week's Reflection

Areas to Celebrate:

Areas to Improve:

What did I learn

This Week's Planning

Plan for joyful occasions. Joy is your strength, refreshment, energy, and beauty. What are you looking forward to this week? Find something to laugh about and share it.

Projects/Areas of focus this week:

- [ ]
- [ ]
- [ ]
- [ ]
- [ ]
- [ ]
- [ ]

AREAS TO SIMPLIFY – where to set godly boundaries

	What is important	What is not important	Why	What are Facts/Feelings	Benefits of continuing/not continuing	Pray about possibilities and solutions
Time						
Energy						
Money						
Relationships						
Possessions						

FASTING: Take authority over what controls me; lean on God; keep Christ-focused
What to fast:
Time to fast:
How to fast:
Check motives:

ADDITIONAL REFLECTION

Date:

SCRIPTURE – DRAW CLOSER TO THE KING OF KINGS: Use your name in the place of a character in the scripture you're reading; imagine yourself in that time, using all 5 senses. Pray scripture back to God. Write the scripture down, read it, repeat it out loud throughout the day, memorize it, and meditate on it.

WORSHIP – PRAISE HIM FOR WHO HE IS: How will you glorify and magnify Him today? There is no room here for making personal petitions.

PURE HEART – ASK HIM TO PURIFY YOUR MIND AND HEART: Replace negative thoughts with higher thoughts. God's thoughts are noble, pure, lovely, excellent, right, true, and admirable. Ask God to reveal areas in your life that grieve the Holy Spirit. Confess with a contrite heart and receive forgiveness. As you confess, turn your palms up and release your sin, worry, and anxiety over to God. Now turn your palms down and receive God's love, mercy, favor, and grace.

THANKFULNESS – NAME THOSE THINGS YOU ARE THANKFUL FOR: There's always something to be grateful for. Name them one by one and come back often to rekindle the joy of each one of them.

O

O

O

O

O

O

O

REFLECTION & REVELATION – PRACTICE LISTENING FOR GOD: God promises that if you draw near to Him, He will tell you things you do not know. Who does God bring to mind? Where is God leading you? Reflect on God's perspective.	TASKS
PRAYER – YOU HAVE NOT BECAUSE YOU ASK NOT: Pray for family, friends, relationships, unity, community, world, church, favor, wisdom, God's will, work, and your future. Pray about anything and everything, without ceasing.	
OBEDIENCE – STAND, SHARE, SERVE: Take steps of faith, and obey promptly. The level of miracles in your life will be directly related to your level of obedience. Faith without works is dead. You have an assignment, a destiny to fulfill.	
	6 am
	7 am
	8 am
	9 am
	10 am
	11 am
	12 pm
	1 pm
	2 pm
	3 pm
	4 pm
	5 pm
	6 pm
	7 pm
	8 pm
	9 pm

Date:

SCRIPTURE – DRAW CLOSER TO THE KING OF KINGS: Use your name in the place of a character in the scripture you're reading; imagine yourself in that time, using all 5 senses. Pray scripture back to God. Write the scripture down, read it, repeat it out loud throughout the day, memorize it, and meditate on it.

WORSHIP – PRAISE HIM FOR WHO HE IS: How will you glorify and magnify Him today? There is no room here for making personal petitions.

PURE HEART – ASK HIM TO PURIFY YOUR MIND AND HEART: Replace negative thoughts with higher thoughts. God's thoughts are noble, pure, lovely, excellent, right, true, and admirable. Ask God to reveal areas in your life that grieve the Holy Spirit. Confess with a contrite heart and receive forgiveness. As you confess, turn your palms up and release your sin, worry, and anxiety over to God. Now turn your palms down and receive God's love, mercy, favor, and grace.

THANKFULNESS – NAME THOSE THINGS YOU ARE THANKFUL FOR: There's always something to be grateful for. Name them one by one and come back often to rekindle the joy of each one of them.

O

O

O

O

O

O

O

REFLECTION & REVELATION – PRACTICE LISTENING FOR GOD: God promises that if you draw near to Him, He will tell you things you do not know. Who does God bring to mind? Where is God leading you? Reflect on God's perspective.	TASKS
PRAYER – YOU HAVE NOT BECAUSE YOU ASK NOT: Pray for family, friends, relationships, unity, community, world, church, favor, wisdom, God's will, work, and your future. Pray about anything and everything, without ceasing.	
OBEDIENCE – STAND, SHARE, SERVE: Take steps of faith, and obey promptly. The level of miracles in your life will be directly related to your level of obedience. Faith without works is dead. You have an assignment, a destiny to fulfill.	
	6 am
	7 am
	8 am
	9 am
	10 am
	11 am
	12 pm
	1 pm
	2 pm
	3 pm
	4 pm
	5 pm
	6 pm
	7 pm
	8 pm
	9 pm

Date:

SCRIPTURE – DRAW CLOSER TO THE KING OF KINGS: Use your name in the place of a character in the scripture you're reading; imagine yourself in that time, using all 5 senses. Pray scripture back to God. Write the scripture down, read it, repeat it out loud throughout the day, memorize it, and meditate on it.

WORSHIP – PRAISE HIM FOR WHO HE IS: How will you glorify and magnify Him today? There is no room here for making personal petitions.

PURE HEART – ASK HIM TO PURIFY YOUR MIND AND HEART: Replace negative thoughts with higher thoughts. God's thoughts are noble, pure, lovely, excellent, right, true, and admirable. Ask God to reveal areas in your life that grieve the Holy Spirit. Confess with a contrite heart and receive forgiveness. As you confess, turn your palms up and release your sin, worry, and anxiety over to God. Now turn your palms down and receive God's love, mercy, favor, and grace.

THANKFULNESS – NAME THOSE THINGS YOU ARE THANKFUL FOR: There's always something to be grateful for. Name them one by one and come back often to rekindle the joy of each one of them.

O

O

O

O

O

O

O

REFLECTION & REVELATION – PRACTICE LISTENING FOR GOD: God promises that if you draw near to Him, He will tell you things you do not know. Who does God bring to mind? Where is God leading you? Reflect on God's perspective.	TASKS
PRAYER – YOU HAVE NOT BECAUSE YOU ASK NOT: Pray for family, friends, relationships, unity, community, world, church, favor, wisdom, God's will, work, and your future. Pray about anything and everything, without ceasing.	
OBEDIENCE – STAND, SHARE, SERVE: Take steps of faith, and obey promptly. The level of miracles in your life will be directly related to your level of obedience. Faith without works is dead. You have an assignment, a destiny to fulfill.	
	6 am
	7 am
	8 am
	9 am
	10 am
	11 am
	12 pm
	1 pm
	2 pm
	3 pm
	4 pm
	5 pm
	6 pm
	7 pm
	8 pm
	9 pm

Date:

SCRIPTURE – DRAW CLOSER TO THE KING OF KINGS: Use your name in the place of a character in the scripture you're reading; imagine yourself in that time, using all 5 senses. Pray scripture back to God. Write the scripture down, read it, repeat it out loud throughout the day, memorize it, and meditate on it.

WORSHIP – PRAISE HIM FOR WHO HE IS: How will you glorify and magnify Him today? There is no room here for making personal petitions.

PURE HEART – ASK HIM TO PURIFY YOUR MIND AND HEART: Replace negative thoughts with higher thoughts. God's thoughts are noble, pure, lovely, excellent, right, true, and admirable. Ask God to reveal areas in your life that grieve the Holy Spirit. Confess with a contrite heart and receive forgiveness. As you confess, turn your palms up and release your sin, worry, and anxiety over to God. Now turn your palms down and receive God's love, mercy, favor, and grace.

THANKFULNESS – NAME THOSE THINGS YOU ARE THANKFUL FOR: There's always something to be grateful for. Name them one by one and come back often to rekindle the joy of each one of them.

O

O

O

O

O

O

O

REFLECTION & REVELATION – PRACTICE LISTENING FOR GOD: God promises that if you draw near to Him, He will tell you things you do not know. Who does God bring to mind? Where is God leading you? Reflect on God's perspective.	TASKS
PRAYER – YOU HAVE NOT BECAUSE YOU ASK NOT: Pray for family, friends, relationships, unity, community, world, church, favor, wisdom, God's will, work, and your future. Pray about anything and everything, without ceasing.	
OBEDIENCE – STAND, SHARE, SERVE: Take steps of faith, and obey promptly. The level of miracles in your life will be directly related to your level of obedience. Faith without works is dead. You have an assignment, a destiny to fulfill.	
	6 am
	7 am
	8 am
	9 am
	10 am
	11 am
	12 pm
	1 pm
	2 pm
	3 pm
	4 pm
	5 pm
	6 pm
	7 pm
	8 pm
	9 pm

Date:

SCRIPTURE – DRAW CLOSER TO THE KING OF KINGS: Use your name in the place of a character in the scripture you're reading; imagine yourself in that time, using all 5 senses. Pray scripture back to God. Write the scripture down, read it, repeat it out loud throughout the day, memorize it, and meditate on it.

WORSHIP – PRAISE HIM FOR WHO HE IS: How will you glorify and magnify Him today? There is no room here for making personal petitions.

PURE HEART – ASK HIM TO PURIFY YOUR MIND AND HEART: Replace negative thoughts with higher thoughts. God's thoughts are noble, pure, lovely, excellent, right, true, and admirable. Ask God to reveal areas in your life that grieve the Holy Spirit. Confess with a contrite heart and receive forgiveness. As you confess, turn your palms up and release your sin, worry, and anxiety over to God. Now turn your palms down and receive God's love, mercy, favor, and grace.

THANKFULNESS – NAME THOSE THINGS YOU ARE THANKFUL FOR: There's always something to be grateful for. Name them one by one and come back often to rekindle the joy of each one of them.

O

O

O

O

O

O

O

REFLECTION & REVELATION – PRACTICE LISTENING FOR GOD: God promises that if you draw near to Him, He will tell you things you do not know. Who does God bring to mind? Where is God leading you? Reflect on God's perspective.	TASKS
PRAYER – YOU HAVE NOT BECAUSE YOU ASK NOT: Pray for family, friends, relationships, unity, community, world, church, favor, wisdom, God's will, work, and your future. Pray about anything and everything, without ceasing.	
OBEDIENCE – STAND, SHARE, SERVE: Take steps of faith, and obey promptly. The level of miracles in your life will be directly related to your level of obedience. Faith without works is dead. You have an assignment, a destiny to fulfill.	
	6 am
	7 am
	8 am
	9 am
	10 am
	11 am
	12 pm
	1 pm
	2 pm
	3 pm
	4 pm
	5 pm
	6 pm
	7 pm
	8 pm
	9 pm

Date:

SCRIPTURE – DRAW CLOSER TO THE KING OF KINGS: Use your name in the place of a character in the scripture you're reading; imagine yourself in that time, using all 5 senses. Pray scripture back to God. Write the scripture down, read it, repeat it out loud throughout the day, memorize it, and meditate on it.

WORSHIP – PRAISE HIM FOR WHO HE IS: How will you glorify and magnify Him today? There is no room here for making personal petitions.

PURE HEART – ASK HIM TO PURIFY YOUR MIND AND HEART: Replace negative thoughts with higher thoughts. God's thoughts are noble, pure, lovely, excellent, right, true, and admirable. Ask God to reveal areas in your life that grieve the Holy Spirit. Confess with a contrite heart and receive forgiveness. As you confess, turn your palms up and release your sin, worry, and anxiety over to God. Now turn your palms down and receive God's love, mercy, favor, and grace.

THANKFULNESS – NAME THOSE THINGS YOU ARE THANKFUL FOR: There's always something to be grateful for. Name them one by one and come back often to rekindle the joy of each one of them.

O

O

O

O

O

O

O

	TASKS
REFLECTION & REVELATION – PRACTICE LISTENING FOR GOD: God promises that if you draw near to Him, He will tell you things you do not know. Who does God bring to mind? Where is God leading you? Reflect on God's perspective.	
PRAYER – YOU HAVE NOT BECAUSE YOU ASK NOT: Pray for family, friends, relationships, unity, community, world, church, favor, wisdom, God's will, work, and your future. Pray about anything and everything, without ceasing.	
OBEDIENCE – STAND, SHARE, SERVE: Take steps of faith, and obey promptly. The level of miracles in your life will be directly related to your level of obedience. Faith without works is dead. You have an assignment, a destiny to fulfill.	
	6 am
	7 am
	8 am
	9 am
	10 am
	11 am
	12 pm
	1 pm
	2 pm
	3 pm
	4 pm
	5 pm
	6 pm
	7 pm
	8 pm
	9 pm

Date:

SCRIPTURE – DRAW CLOSER TO THE KING OF KINGS: Use your name in the place of a character in the scripture you're reading; imagine yourself in that time, using all 5 senses. Pray scripture back to God. Write the scripture down, read it, repeat it out loud throughout the day, memorize it, and meditate on it.

WORSHIP – PRAISE HIM FOR WHO HE IS: How will you glorify and magnify Him today? There is no room here for making personal petitions.

PURE HEART – ASK HIM TO PURIFY YOUR MIND AND HEART: Replace negative thoughts with higher thoughts. God's thoughts are noble, pure, lovely, excellent, right, true, and admirable. Ask God to reveal areas in your life that grieve the Holy Spirit. Confess with a contrite heart and receive forgiveness. As you confess, turn your palms up and release your sin, worry, and anxiety over to God. Now turn your palms down and receive God's love, mercy, favor, and grace.

THANKFULNESS – NAME THOSE THINGS YOU ARE THANKFUL FOR: There's always something to be grateful for. Name them one by one and come back often to rekindle the joy of each one of them.

O

O

O

O

O

O

O

	TASKS
REFLECTION & REVELATION – PRACTICE LISTENING FOR GOD: God promises that if you draw near to Him, He will tell you things you do not know. Who does God bring to mind? Where is God leading you? Reflect on God's perspective.	
PRAYER – YOU HAVE NOT BECAUSE YOU ASK NOT: Pray for family, friends, relationships, unity, community, world, church, favor, wisdom, God's will, work, and your future. Pray about anything and everything, without ceasing.	
OBEDIENCE – STAND, SHARE, SERVE: Take steps of faith, and obey promptly. The level of miracles in your life will be directly related to your level of obedience. Faith without works is dead. You have an assignment, a destiny to fulfill.	
	6 am
	7 am
	8 am
	9 am
	10 am
	11 am
	12 pm
	1 pm
	2 pm
	3 pm
	4 pm
	5 pm
	6 pm
	7 pm
	8 pm
	9 pm

WEEKLY FOCUS

Last Week's Reflection
Areas to Celebrate:
Areas to Improve:
What did I learn

This Week's Planning
Plan for joyful occasions. Joy is your strength, refreshment, energy, and beauty. What are you looking forward to this week? Find something to laugh about and share it.
Projects/Areas of focus this week:

Projects/Areas of focus this week:

- ☐
- ☐
- ☐
- ☐
- ☐
- ☐
- ☐

AREAS TO SIMPLIFY – where to set godly boundaries

	What is important	What is not important	Why	What are Facts/Feelings	Benefits of continuing/not continuing	Pray about possibilities and solutions
Time						
Energy						
Money						
Relationships						
Possessions						

FASTING: Take authority over what controls me; lean on God; keep Christ-focused
What to fast:
Time to fast:
How to fast:
Check motives:

Additional Reflection

Date:

SCRIPTURE – DRAW CLOSER TO THE KING OF KINGS: Use your name in the place of a character in the scripture you're reading; imagine yourself in that time, using all 5 senses. Pray scripture back to God. Write the scripture down, read it, repeat it out loud throughout the day, memorize it, and meditate on it.

_____
_____
_____
_____
_____
_____
_____
_____
_____
_____
_____
_____
_____

WORSHIP – PRAISE HIM FOR WHO HE IS: How will you glorify and magnify Him today? There is no room here for making personal petitions.

_____
_____
_____
_____

PURE HEART – ASK HIM TO PURIFY YOUR MIND AND HEART: Replace negative thoughts with higher thoughts. God's thoughts are noble, pure, lovely, excellent, right, true, and admirable. Ask God to reveal areas in your life that grieve the Holy Spirit. Confess with a contrite heart and receive forgiveness. As you confess, turn your palms up and release your sin, worry, and anxiety over to God. Now turn your palms down and receive God's love, mercy, favor, and grace.

_____
_____
_____

THANKFULNESS – NAME THOSE THINGS YOU ARE THANKFUL FOR: There's always something to be grateful for. Name them one by one and come back often to rekindle the joy of each one of them.

O
O
O
O
O
O
O

REFLECTION & REVELATION – PRACTICE LISTENING FOR GOD: God promises that if you draw near to Him, He will tell you things you do not know. Who does God bring to mind? Where is God leading you? Reflect on God's perspective.	TASKS
PRAYER – YOU HAVE NOT BECAUSE YOU ASK NOT: Pray for family, friends, relationships, unity, community, world, church, favor, wisdom, God's will, work, and your future. Pray about anything and everything, without ceasing.	
OBEDIENCE – STAND, SHARE, SERVE: Take steps of faith, and obey promptly. The level of miracles in your life will be directly related to your level of obedience. Faith without works is dead. You have an assignment, a destiny to fulfill.	
	6 am
	7 am
	8 am
	9 am
	10 am
	11 am
	12 pm
	1 pm
	2 pm
	3 pm
	4 pm
	5 pm
	6 pm
	7 pm
	8 pm
	9 pm

Date:

SCRIPTURE – DRAW CLOSER TO THE KING OF KINGS: Use your name in the place of a character in the scripture you're reading; imagine yourself in that time, using all 5 senses. Pray scripture back to God. Write the scripture down, read it, repeat it out loud throughout the day, memorize it, and meditate on it.

WORSHIP – PRAISE HIM FOR WHO HE IS: How will you glorify and magnify Him today? There is no room here for making personal petitions.

PURE HEART – ASK HIM TO PURIFY YOUR MIND AND HEART: Replace negative thoughts with higher thoughts. God's thoughts are noble, pure, lovely, excellent, right, true, and admirable. Ask God to reveal areas in your life that grieve the Holy Spirit. Confess with a contrite heart and receive forgiveness. As you confess, turn your palms up and release your sin, worry, and anxiety over to God. Now turn your palms down and receive God's love, mercy, favor, and grace.

THANKFULNESS – NAME THOSE THINGS YOU ARE THANKFUL FOR: There's always something to be grateful for. Name them one by one and come back often to rekindle the joy of each one of them.

O

O

O

O

O

O

O

REFLECTION & REVELATION – PRACTICE LISTENING FOR GOD: God promises that if you draw near to Him, He will tell you things you do not know. Who does God bring to mind? Where is God leading you? Reflect on God's perspective.	TASKS
PRAYER – YOU HAVE NOT BECAUSE YOU ASK NOT: Pray for family, friends, relationships, unity, community, world, church, favor, wisdom, God's will, work, and your future. Pray about anything and everything, without ceasing.	
OBEDIENCE – STAND, SHARE, SERVE: Take steps of faith, and obey promptly. The level of miracles in your life will be directly related to your level of obedience. Faith without works is dead. You have an assignment, a destiny to fulfill.	
	6 am
	7 am
	8 am
	9 am
	10 am
	11 am
	12 pm
	1 pm
	2 pm
	3 pm
	4 pm
	5 pm
	6 pm
	7 pm
	8 pm
	9 pm

Date:

SCRIPTURE – DRAW CLOSER TO THE KING OF KINGS: Use your name in the place of a character in the scripture you're reading; imagine yourself in that time, using all 5 senses. Pray scripture back to God. Write the scripture down, read it, repeat it out loud throughout the day, memorize it, and meditate on it.

WORSHIP – PRAISE HIM FOR WHO HE IS: How will you glorify and magnify Him today? There is no room here for making personal petitions.

PURE HEART – ASK HIM TO PURIFY YOUR MIND AND HEART: Replace negative thoughts with higher thoughts. God's thoughts are noble, pure, lovely, excellent, right, true, and admirable. Ask God to reveal areas in your life that grieve the Holy Spirit. Confess with a contrite heart and receive forgiveness. As you confess, turn your palms up and release your sin, worry, and anxiety over to God. Now turn your palms down and receive God's love, mercy, favor, and grace.

THANKFULNESS – NAME THOSE THINGS YOU ARE THANKFUL FOR: There's always something to be grateful for. Name them one by one and come back often to rekindle the joy of each one of them.

O

O

O

O

O

O

O

REFLECTION & REVELATION – PRACTICE LISTENING FOR GOD: God promises that if you draw near to Him, He will tell you things you do not know. Who does God bring to mind? Where is God leading you? Reflect on God's perspective.	TASKS
PRAYER – YOU HAVE NOT BECAUSE YOU ASK NOT: Pray for family, friends, relationships, unity, community, world, church, favor, wisdom, God's will, work, and your future. Pray about anything and everything, without ceasing.	
OBEDIENCE – STAND, SHARE, SERVE: Take steps of faith, and obey promptly. The level of miracles in your life will be directly related to your level of obedience. Faith without works is dead. You have an assignment, a destiny to fulfill.	
	6 am
	7 am
	8 am
	9 am
	10 am
	11 am
	12 pm
	1 pm
	2 pm
	3 pm
	4 pm
	5 pm
	6 pm
	7 pm
	8 pm
	9 pm

Date:

SCRIPTURE – DRAW CLOSER TO THE KING OF KINGS: Use your name in the place of a character in the scripture you're reading; imagine yourself in that time, using all 5 senses. Pray scripture back to God. Write the scripture down, read it, repeat it out loud throughout the day, memorize it, and meditate on it.

_____
_____
_____
_____
_____
_____
_____
_____
_____
_____
_____
_____
_____
_____

WORSHIP – PRAISE HIM FOR WHO HE IS: How will you glorify and magnify Him today? There is no room here for making personal petitions.

_____
_____
_____
_____

PURE HEART – ASK HIM TO PURIFY YOUR MIND AND HEART: Replace negative thoughts with higher thoughts. God's thoughts are noble, pure, lovely, excellent, right, true, and admirable. Ask God to reveal areas in your life that grieve the Holy Spirit. Confess with a contrite heart and receive forgiveness. As you confess, turn your palms up and release your sin, worry, and anxiety over to God. Now turn your palms down and receive God's love, mercy, favor, and grace.

_____
_____
_____

THANKFULNESS – NAME THOSE THINGS YOU ARE THANKFUL FOR: There's always something to be grateful for. Name them one by one and come back often to rekindle the joy of each one of them.

O

O

O

O

O

O

O

REFLECTION & REVELATION – PRACTICE LISTENING FOR GOD: God promises that if you draw near to Him, He will tell you things you do not know. Who does God bring to mind? Where is God leading you? Reflect on God's perspective.	TASKS
PRAYER – YOU HAVE NOT BECAUSE YOU ASK NOT: Pray for family, friends, relationships, unity, community, world, church, favor, wisdom, God's will, work, and your future. Pray about anything and everything, without ceasing.	
OBEDIENCE – STAND, SHARE, SERVE: Take steps of faith, and obey promptly. The level of miracles in your life will be directly related to your level of obedience. Faith without works is dead. You have an assignment, a destiny to fulfill.	
	6 am
	7 am
	8 am
	9 am
	10 am
	11 am
	12 pm
	1 pm
	2 pm
	3 pm
	4 pm
	5 pm
	6 pm
	7 pm
	8 pm
	9 pm

Date:

SCRIPTURE – DRAW CLOSER TO THE KING OF KINGS: Use your name in the place of a character in the scripture you're reading; imagine yourself in that time, using all 5 senses. Pray scripture back to God. Write the scripture down, read it, repeat it out loud throughout the day, memorize it, and meditate on it.

WORSHIP – PRAISE HIM FOR WHO HE IS: How will you glorify and magnify Him today? There is no room here for making personal petitions.

PURE HEART – ASK HIM TO PURIFY YOUR MIND AND HEART: Replace negative thoughts with higher thoughts. God's thoughts are noble, pure, lovely, excellent, right, true, and admirable. Ask God to reveal areas in your life that grieve the Holy Spirit. Confess with a contrite heart and receive forgiveness. As you confess, turn your palms up and release your sin, worry, and anxiety over to God. Now turn your palms down and receive God's love, mercy, favor, and grace.

THANKFULNESS – NAME THOSE THINGS YOU ARE THANKFUL FOR: There's always something to be grateful for. Name them one by one and come back often to rekindle the joy of each one of them.

O

O

O

O

O

O

O

REFLECTION & REVELATION – PRACTICE LISTENING FOR GOD: God promises that if you draw near to Him, He will tell you things you do not know. Who does God bring to mind? Where is God leading you? Reflect on God's perspective.	TASKS
PRAYER – YOU HAVE NOT BECAUSE YOU ASK NOT: Pray for family, friends, relationships, unity, community, world, church, favor, wisdom, God's will, work, and your future. Pray about anything and everything, without ceasing.	
OBEDIENCE – STAND, SHARE, SERVE: Take steps of faith, and obey promptly. The level of miracles in your life will be directly related to your level of obedience. Faith without works is dead. You have an assignment, a destiny to fulfill.	
	6 am
	7 am
	8 am
	9 am
	10 am
	11 am
	12 pm
	1 pm
	2 pm
	3 pm
	4 pm
	5 pm
	6 pm
	7 pm
	8 pm
	9 pm

Date:

SCRIPTURE – DRAW CLOSER TO THE KING OF KINGS: Use your name in the place of a character in the scripture you're reading; imagine yourself in that time, using all 5 senses. Pray scripture back to God. Write the scripture down, read it, repeat it out loud throughout the day, memorize it, and meditate on it.

WORSHIP – PRAISE HIM FOR WHO HE IS: How will you glorify and magnify Him today? There is no room here for making personal petitions.

PURE HEART – ASK HIM TO PURIFY YOUR MIND AND HEART: Replace negative thoughts with higher thoughts. God's thoughts are noble, pure, lovely, excellent, right, true, and admirable. Ask God to reveal areas in your life that grieve the Holy Spirit. Confess with a contrite heart and receive forgiveness. As you confess, turn your palms up and release your sin, worry, and anxiety over to God. Now turn your palms down and receive God's love, mercy, favor, and grace.

THANKFULNESS – NAME THOSE THINGS YOU ARE THANKFUL FOR: There's always something to be grateful for. Name them one by one and come back often to rekindle the joy of each one of them.

O

O

O

O

O

O

O

REFLECTION & REVELATION – PRACTICE LISTENING FOR GOD: God promises that if you draw near to Him, He will tell you things you do not know. Who does God bring to mind? Where is God leading you? Reflect on God's perspective.	TASKS
PRAYER – YOU HAVE NOT BECAUSE YOU ASK NOT: Pray for family, friends, relationships, unity, community, world, church, favor, wisdom, God's will, work, and your future. Pray about anything and everything, without ceasing.	
OBEDIENCE – STAND, SHARE, SERVE: Take steps of faith, and obey promptly. The level of miracles in your life will be directly related to your level of obedience. Faith without works is dead. You have an assignment, a destiny to fulfill.	
	6 am
	7 am
	8 am
	9 am
	10 am
	11 am
	12 pm
	1 pm
	2 pm
	3 pm
	4 pm
	5 pm
	6 pm
	7 pm
	8 pm
	9 pm

Date:

SCRIPTURE – DRAW CLOSER TO THE KING OF KINGS: Use your name in the place of a character in the scripture you're reading; imagine yourself in that time, using all 5 senses. Pray scripture back to God. Write the scripture down, read it, repeat it out loud throughout the day, memorize it, and meditate on it.

WORSHIP – PRAISE HIM FOR WHO HE IS: How will you glorify and magnify Him today? There is no room here for making personal petitions.

PURE HEART – ASK HIM TO PURIFY YOUR MIND AND HEART: Replace negative thoughts with higher thoughts. God's thoughts are noble, pure, lovely, excellent, right, true, and admirable. Ask God to reveal areas in your life that grieve the Holy Spirit. Confess with a contrite heart and receive forgiveness. As you confess, turn your palms up and release your sin, worry, and anxiety over to God. Now turn your palms down and receive God's love, mercy, favor, and grace.

THANKFULNESS – NAME THOSE THINGS YOU ARE THANKFUL FOR: There's always something to be grateful for. Name them one by one and come back often to rekindle the joy of each one of them.

O

O

O

O

O

O

O

REFLECTION & REVELATION – PRACTICE LISTENING FOR GOD: God promises that if you draw near to Him, He will tell you things you do not know. Who does God bring to mind? Where is God leading you? Reflect on God's perspective.	TASKS
PRAYER – YOU HAVE NOT BECAUSE YOU ASK NOT: Pray for family, friends, relationships, unity, community, world, church, favor, wisdom, God's will, work, and your future. Pray about anything and everything, without ceasing.	
OBEDIENCE – STAND, SHARE, SERVE: Take steps of faith, and obey promptly. The level of miracles in your life will be directly related to your level of obedience. Faith without works is dead. You have an assignment, a destiny to fulfill.	
	6 am
	7 am
	8 am
	9 am
	10 am
	11 am
	12 pm
	1 pm
	2 pm
	3 pm
	4 pm
	5 pm
	6 pm
	7 pm
	8 pm
	9 pm

WEEKLY FOCUS

Last Week's Reflection
Areas to Celebrate:
Areas to Improve:
What did I learn

This Week's Planning
Plan for joyful occasions. Joy is your strength, refreshment, energy, and beauty. What are you looking forward to this week? Find something to laugh about and share it.
Projects/Areas of focus this week:

AREAS TO SIMPLIFY – where to set godly boundaries

	What is important	What is not important	Why	What are Facts/Feelings	Benefits of continuing/not continuing	Pray about possibilities and solutions
Time						
Energy						
Money						
Relationships						
Possessions						

FASTING: Take authority over what controls me; lean on God; keep Christ-focused
What to fast:
Time to fast:
How to fast:
Check motives:

ADDITIONAL REFLECTION

Date:

SCRIPTURE – DRAW CLOSER TO THE KING OF KINGS: Use your name in the place of a character in the scripture you're reading; imagine yourself in that time, using all 5 senses. Pray scripture back to God. Write the scripture down, read it, repeat it out loud throughout the day, memorize it, and meditate on it.

WORSHIP – PRAISE HIM FOR WHO HE IS: How will you glorify and magnify Him today? There is no room here for making personal petitions.

PURE HEART – ASK HIM TO PURIFY YOUR MIND AND HEART: Replace negative thoughts with higher thoughts. God's thoughts are noble, pure, lovely, excellent, right, true, and admirable. Ask God to reveal areas in your life that grieve the Holy Spirit. Confess with a contrite heart and receive forgiveness. As you confess, turn your palms up and release your sin, worry, and anxiety over to God. Now turn your palms down and receive God's love, mercy, favor, and grace.

THANKFULNESS – NAME THOSE THINGS YOU ARE THANKFUL FOR: There's always something to be grateful for. Name them one by one and come back often to rekindle the joy of each one of them.

O

O

O

O

O

O

O

	TASKS
REFLECTION & REVELATION – PRACTICE LISTENING FOR GOD: God promises that if you draw near to Him, He will tell you things you do not know. Who does God bring to mind? Where is God leading you? Reflect on God's perspective.	
PRAYER – YOU HAVE NOT BECAUSE YOU ASK NOT: Pray for family, friends, relationships, unity, community, world, church, favor, wisdom, God's will, work, and your future. Pray about anything and everything, without ceasing.	
OBEDIENCE – STAND, SHARE, SERVE: Take steps of faith, and obey promptly. The level of miracles in your life will be directly related to your level of obedience. Faith without works is dead. You have an assignment, a destiny to fulfill.	
	6 am
	7 am
	8 am
	9 am
	10 am
	11 am
	12 pm
	1 pm
	2 pm
	3 pm
	4 pm
	5 pm
	6 pm
	7 pm
	8 pm
	9 pm

Date:

SCRIPTURE – DRAW CLOSER TO THE KING OF KINGS: Use your name in the place of a character in the scripture you're reading; imagine yourself in that time, using all 5 senses. Pray scripture back to God. Write the scripture down, read it, repeat it out loud throughout the day, memorize it, and meditate on it.

WORSHIP – PRAISE HIM FOR WHO HE IS: How will you glorify and magnify Him today? There is no room here for making personal petitions.

PURE HEART – ASK HIM TO PURIFY YOUR MIND AND HEART: Replace negative thoughts with higher thoughts. God's thoughts are noble, pure, lovely, excellent, right, true, and admirable. Ask God to reveal areas in your life that grieve the Holy Spirit. Confess with a contrite heart and receive forgiveness. As you confess, turn your palms up and release your sin, worry, and anxiety over to God. Now turn your palms down and receive God's love, mercy, favor, and grace.

THANKFULNESS – NAME THOSE THINGS YOU ARE THANKFUL FOR: There's always something to be grateful for. Name them one by one and come back often to rekindle the joy of each one of them.

O

O

O

O

O

O

O

	TASKS
REFLECTION & REVELATION – PRACTICE LISTENING FOR GOD: God promises that if you draw near to Him, He will tell you things you do not know. Who does God bring to mind? Where is God leading you? Reflect on God's perspective.	
PRAYER – YOU HAVE NOT BECAUSE YOU ASK NOT: Pray for family, friends, relationships, unity, community, world, church, favor, wisdom, God's will, work, and your future. Pray about anything and everything, without ceasing.	
OBEDIENCE – STAND, SHARE, SERVE: Take steps of faith, and obey promptly. The level of miracles in your life will be directly related to your level of obedience. Faith without works is dead. You have an assignment, a destiny to fulfill.	
	6 am
	7 am
	8 am
	9 am
	10 am
	11 am
	12 pm
	1 pm
	2 pm
	3 pm
	4 pm
	5 pm
	6 pm
	7 pm
	8 pm
	9 pm

Date:

SCRIPTURE – DRAW CLOSER TO THE KING OF KINGS: Use your name in the place of a character in the scripture you're reading; imagine yourself in that time, using all 5 senses. Pray scripture back to God. Write the scripture down, read it, repeat it out loud throughout the day, memorize it, and meditate on it.

WORSHIP – PRAISE HIM FOR WHO HE IS: How will you glorify and magnify Him today? There is no room here for making personal petitions.

PURE HEART – ASK HIM TO PURIFY YOUR MIND AND HEART: Replace negative thoughts with higher thoughts. God's thoughts are noble, pure, lovely, excellent, right, true, and admirable. Ask God to reveal areas in your life that grieve the Holy Spirit. Confess with a contrite heart and receive forgiveness. As you confess, turn your palms up and release your sin, worry, and anxiety over to God. Now turn your palms down and receive God's love, mercy, favor, and grace.

THANKFULNESS – NAME THOSE THINGS YOU ARE THANKFUL FOR: There's always something to be grateful for. Name them one by one and come back often to rekindle the joy of each one of them.

O

O

O

O

O

O

O

REFLECTION & REVELATION – PRACTICE LISTENING FOR GOD: God promises that if you draw near to Him, He will tell you things you do not know. Who does God bring to mind? Where is God leading you? Reflect on God's perspective.	TASKS
PRAYER – YOU HAVE NOT BECAUSE YOU ASK NOT: Pray for family, friends, relationships, unity, community, world, church, favor, wisdom, God's will, work, and your future. Pray about anything and everything, without ceasing.	
OBEDIENCE – STAND, SHARE, SERVE: Take steps of faith, and obey promptly. The level of miracles in your life will be directly related to your level of obedience. Faith without works is dead. You have an assignment, a destiny to fulfill.	
	6 am
	7 am
	8 am
	9 am
	10 am
	11 am
	12 pm
	1 pm
	2 pm
	3 pm
	4 pm
	5 pm
	6 pm
	7 pm
	8 pm
	9 pm

Date:

SCRIPTURE – DRAW CLOSER TO THE KING OF KINGS: Use your name in the place of a character in the scripture you're reading; imagine yourself in that time, using all 5 senses. Pray scripture back to God. Write the scripture down, read it, repeat it out loud throughout the day, memorize it, and meditate on it.

WORSHIP – PRAISE HIM FOR WHO HE IS: How will you glorify and magnify Him today? There is no room here for making personal petitions.

PURE HEART – ASK HIM TO PURIFY YOUR MIND AND HEART: Replace negative thoughts with higher thoughts. God's thoughts are noble, pure, lovely, excellent, right, true, and admirable. Ask God to reveal areas in your life that grieve the Holy Spirit. Confess with a contrite heart and receive forgiveness. As you confess, turn your palms up and release your sin, worry, and anxiety over to God. Now turn your palms down and receive God's love, mercy, favor, and grace.

THANKFULNESS – NAME THOSE THINGS YOU ARE THANKFUL FOR: There's always something to be grateful for. Name them one by one and come back often to rekindle the joy of each one of them.

O

O

O

O

O

O

O

	TASKS
REFLECTION & REVELATION – PRACTICE LISTENING FOR GOD: God promises that if you draw near to Him, He will tell you things you do not know. Who does God bring to mind? Where is God leading you? Reflect on God's perspective.	
PRAYER – YOU HAVE NOT BECAUSE YOU ASK NOT: Pray for family, friends, relationships, unity, community, world, church, favor, wisdom, God's will, work, and your future. Pray about anything and everything, without ceasing.	
OBEDIENCE – STAND, SHARE, SERVE: Take steps of faith, and obey promptly. The level of miracles in your life will be directly related to your level of obedience. Faith without works is dead. You have an assignment, a destiny to fulfill.	
	6 am
	7 am
	8 am
	9 am
	10 am
	11 am
	12 pm
	1 pm
	2 pm
	3 pm
	4 pm
	5 pm
	6 pm
	7 pm
	8 pm
	9 pm

Date:

SCRIPTURE – DRAW CLOSER TO THE KING OF KINGS: Use your name in the place of a character in the scripture you're reading; imagine yourself in that time, using all 5 senses. Pray scripture back to God. Write the scripture down, read it, repeat it out loud throughout the day, memorize it, and meditate on it.

WORSHIP – PRAISE HIM FOR WHO HE IS: How will you glorify and magnify Him today? There is no room here for making personal petitions.

PURE HEART – ASK HIM TO PURIFY YOUR MIND AND HEART: Replace negative thoughts with higher thoughts. God's thoughts are noble, pure, lovely, excellent, right, true, and admirable. Ask God to reveal areas in your life that grieve the Holy Spirit. Confess with a contrite heart and receive forgiveness. As you confess, turn your palms up and release your sin, worry, and anxiety over to God. Now turn your palms down and receive God's love, mercy, favor, and grace.

THANKFULNESS – NAME THOSE THINGS YOU ARE THANKFUL FOR: There's always something to be grateful for. Name them one by one and come back often to rekindle the joy of each one of them.

O

O

O

O

O

O

O

	TASKS
REFLECTION & REVELATION – PRACTICE LISTENING FOR GOD: God promises that if you draw near to Him, He will tell you things you do not know. Who does God bring to mind? Where is God leading you? Reflect on God's perspective.	
PRAYER – YOU HAVE NOT BECAUSE YOU ASK NOT: Pray for family, friends, relationships, unity, community, world, church, favor, wisdom, God's will, work, and your future. Pray about anything and everything, without ceasing.	
OBEDIENCE – STAND, SHARE, SERVE: Take steps of faith, and obey promptly. The level of miracles in your life will be directly related to your level of obedience. Faith without works is dead. You have an assignment, a destiny to fulfill.	
	6 am
	7 am
	8 am
	9 am
	10 am
	11 am
	12 pm
	1 pm
	2 pm
	3 pm
	4 pm
	5 pm
	6 pm
	7 pm
	8 pm
	9 pm

Date:

SCRIPTURE – DRAW CLOSER TO THE KING OF KINGS: Use your name in the place of a character in the scripture you're reading; imagine yourself in that time, using all 5 senses. Pray scripture back to God. Write the scripture down, read it, repeat it out loud throughout the day, memorize it, and meditate on it.

WORSHIP – PRAISE HIM FOR WHO HE IS: How will you glorify and magnify Him today? There is no room here for making personal petitions.

PURE HEART – ASK HIM TO PURIFY YOUR MIND AND HEART: Replace negative thoughts with higher thoughts. God's thoughts are noble, pure, lovely, excellent, right, true, and admirable. Ask God to reveal areas in your life that grieve the Holy Spirit. Confess with a contrite heart and receive forgiveness. As you confess, turn your palms up and release your sin, worry, and anxiety over to God. Now turn your palms down and receive God's love, mercy, favor, and grace.

THANKFULNESS – NAME THOSE THINGS YOU ARE THANKFUL FOR: There's always something to be grateful for. Name them one by one and come back often to rekindle the joy of each one of them.

O

O

O

O

O

O

O

REFLECTION & REVELATION – PRACTICE LISTENING FOR GOD: God promises that if you draw near to Him, He will tell you things you do not know. Who does God bring to mind? Where is God leading you? Reflect on God's perspective.	TASKS
PRAYER – YOU HAVE NOT BECAUSE YOU ASK NOT: Pray for family, friends, relationships, unity, community, world, church, favor, wisdom, God's will, work, and your future. Pray about anything and everything, without ceasing.	
OBEDIENCE – STAND, SHARE, SERVE: Take steps of faith, and obey promptly. The level of miracles in your life will be directly related to your level of obedience. Faith without works is dead. You have an assignment, a destiny to fulfill.	
	6 am
	7 am
	8 am
	9 am
	10 am
	11 am
	12 pm
	1 pm
	2 pm
	3 pm
	4 pm
	5 pm
	6 pm
	7 pm
	8 pm
	9 pm

Date:

SCRIPTURE – DRAW CLOSER TO THE KING OF KINGS: Use your name in the place of a character in the scripture you're reading; imagine yourself in that time, using all 5 senses. Pray scripture back to God. Write the scripture down, read it, repeat it out loud throughout the day, memorize it, and meditate on it.

WORSHIP – PRAISE HIM FOR WHO HE IS: How will you glorify and magnify Him today? There is no room here for making personal petitions.

PURE HEART – ASK HIM TO PURIFY YOUR MIND AND HEART: Replace negative thoughts with higher thoughts. God's thoughts are noble, pure, lovely, excellent, right, true, and admirable. Ask God to reveal areas in your life that grieve the Holy Spirit. Confess with a contrite heart and receive forgiveness. As you confess, turn your palms up and release your sin, worry, and anxiety over to God. Now turn your palms down and receive God's love, mercy, favor, and grace.

THANKFULNESS – NAME THOSE THINGS YOU ARE THANKFUL FOR: There's always something to be grateful for. Name them one by one and come back often to rekindle the joy of each one of them.

O

O

O

O

O

O

O

REFLECTION & REVELATION – PRACTICE LISTENING FOR GOD: God promises that if you draw near to Him, He will tell you things you do not know. Who does God bring to mind? Where is God leading you? Reflect on God's perspective.	TASKS
PRAYER – YOU HAVE NOT BECAUSE YOU ASK NOT: Pray for family, friends, relationships, unity, community, world, church, favor, wisdom, God's will, work, and your future. Pray about anything and everything, without ceasing.	
OBEDIENCE – STAND, SHARE, SERVE: Take steps of faith, and obey promptly. The level of miracles in your life will be directly related to your level of obedience. Faith without works is dead. You have an assignment, a destiny to fulfill.	
	6 am
	7 am
	8 am
	9 am
	10 am
	11 am
	12 pm
	1 pm
	2 pm
	3 pm
	4 pm
	5 pm
	6 pm
	7 pm
	8 pm
	9 pm

WEEKLY FOCUS

Last Week's Reflection
Areas to Celebrate:
Areas to Improve:
What did I learn

This Week's Planning
Plan for joyful occasions. Joy is your strength, refreshment, energy, and beauty. What are you looking forward to this week? Find something to laugh about and share it.

Projects/Areas of focus this week:

- [ ]
- [ ]
- [ ]
- [ ]
- [ ]
- [ ]
- [ ]

AREAS TO SIMPLIFY – where to set godly boundaries

	What is important	What is not important	Why	What are Facts/Feelings	Benefits of continuing/not continuing	Pray about possibilities and solutions
Time						
Energy						
Money						
Relationships						
Possessions						

FASTING: Take authority over what controls me; lean on God; keep Christ-focused
What to fast:
Time to fast:
How to fast:
Check motives:

Additional Reflection

Date:

SCRIPTURE – DRAW CLOSER TO THE KING OF KINGS: Use your name in the place of a character in the scripture you're reading; imagine yourself in that time, using all 5 senses. Pray scripture back to God. Write the scripture down, read it, repeat it out loud throughout the day, memorize it, and meditate on it.

WORSHIP – PRAISE HIM FOR WHO HE IS: How will you glorify and magnify Him today? There is no room here for making personal petitions.

PURE HEART – ASK HIM TO PURIFY YOUR MIND AND HEART: Replace negative thoughts with higher thoughts. God's thoughts are noble, pure, lovely, excellent, right, true, and admirable. Ask God to reveal areas in your life that grieve the Holy Spirit. Confess with a contrite heart and receive forgiveness. As you confess, turn your palms up and release your sin, worry, and anxiety over to God. Now turn your palms down and receive God's love, mercy, favor, and grace.

THANKFULNESS – NAME THOSE THINGS YOU ARE THANKFUL FOR: There's always something to be grateful for. Name them one by one and come back often to rekindle the joy of each one of them.

O

O

O

O

O

O

O

REFLECTION & REVELATION – PRACTICE LISTENING FOR GOD: God promises that if you draw near to Him, He will tell you things you do not know. Who does God bring to mind? Where is God leading you? Reflect on God's perspective.	TASKS
PRAYER – YOU HAVE NOT BECAUSE YOU ASK NOT: Pray for family, friends, relationships, unity, community, world, church, favor, wisdom, God's will, work, and your future. Pray about anything and everything, without ceasing.	
OBEDIENCE – STAND, SHARE, SERVE: Take steps of faith, and obey promptly. The level of miracles in your life will be directly related to your level of obedience. Faith without works is dead. You have an assignment, a destiny to fulfill.	
	6 am
	7 am
	8 am
	9 am
	10 am
	11 am
	12 pm
	1 pm
	2 pm
	3 pm
	4 pm
	5 pm
	6 pm
	7 pm
	8 pm
	9 pm

Date:

SCRIPTURE – DRAW CLOSER TO THE KING OF KINGS: Use your name in the place of a character in the scripture you're reading; imagine yourself in that time, using all 5 senses. Pray scripture back to God. Write the scripture down, read it, repeat it out loud throughout the day, memorize it, and meditate on it.

_____
_____
_____
_____
_____
_____
_____
_____
_____
_____
_____
_____
_____
_____

WORSHIP – PRAISE HIM FOR WHO HE IS: How will you glorify and magnify Him today? There is no room here for making personal petitions.

_____
_____
_____

PURE HEART – ASK HIM TO PURIFY YOUR MIND AND HEART: Replace negative thoughts with higher thoughts. God's thoughts are noble, pure, lovely, excellent, right, true, and admirable. Ask God to reveal areas in your life that grieve the Holy Spirit. Confess with a contrite heart and receive forgiveness. As you confess, turn your palms up and release your sin, worry, and anxiety over to God. Now turn your palms down and receive God's love, mercy, favor, and grace.

_____
_____
_____

THANKFULNESS – NAME THOSE THINGS YOU ARE THANKFUL FOR: There's always something to be grateful for. Name them one by one and come back often to rekindle the joy of each one of them.

O
O
O
O
O
O
O

REFLECTION & REVELATION – PRACTICE LISTENING FOR GOD: God promises that if you draw near to Him, He will tell you things you do not know. Who does God bring to mind? Where is God leading you? Reflect on God's perspective.	TASKS
PRAYER – YOU HAVE NOT BECAUSE YOU ASK NOT: Pray for family, friends, relationships, unity, community, world, church, favor, wisdom, God's will, work, and your future. Pray about anything and everything, without ceasing.	
OBEDIENCE – STAND, SHARE, SERVE: Take steps of faith, and obey promptly. The level of miracles in your life will be directly related to your level of obedience. Faith without works is dead. You have an assignment, a destiny to fulfill.	
	6 am
	7 am
	8 am
	9 am
	10 am
	11 am
	12 pm
	1 pm
	2 pm
	3 pm
	4 pm
	5 pm
	6 pm
	7 pm
	8 pm
	9 pm

Date:

SCRIPTURE – DRAW CLOSER TO THE KING OF KINGS: Use your name in the place of a character in the scripture you're reading; imagine yourself in that time, using all 5 senses. Pray scripture back to God. Write the scripture down, read it, repeat it out loud throughout the day, memorize it, and meditate on it.

_____
_____
_____
_____
_____
_____
_____
_____
_____
_____
_____
_____
_____

WORSHIP – PRAISE HIM FOR WHO HE IS: How will you glorify and magnify Him today? There is no room here for making personal petitions.

_____
_____
_____
_____

PURE HEART – ASK HIM TO PURIFY YOUR MIND AND HEART: Replace negative thoughts with higher thoughts. God's thoughts are noble, pure, lovely, excellent, right, true, and admirable. Ask God to reveal areas in your life that grieve the Holy Spirit. Confess with a contrite heart and receive forgiveness. As you confess, turn your palms up and release your sin, worry, and anxiety over to God. Now turn your palms down and receive God's love, mercy, favor, and grace.

_____
_____
_____

THANKFULNESS – NAME THOSE THINGS YOU ARE THANKFUL FOR: There's always something to be grateful for. Name them one by one and come back often to rekindle the joy of each one of them.

O
O
O
O
O
O
O

REFLECTION & REVELATION – PRACTICE LISTENING FOR GOD: God promises that if you draw near to Him, He will tell you things you do not know. Who does God bring to mind? Where is God leading you? Reflect on God's perspective.	TASKS
PRAYER – YOU HAVE NOT BECAUSE YOU ASK NOT: Pray for family, friends, relationships, unity, community, world, church, favor, wisdom, God's will, work, and your future. Pray about anything and everything, without ceasing.	
OBEDIENCE – STAND, SHARE, SERVE: Take steps of faith, and obey promptly. The level of miracles in your life will be directly related to your level of obedience. Faith without works is dead. You have an assignment, a destiny to fulfill.	
	6 am
	7 am
	8 am
	9 am
	10 am
	11 am
	12 pm
	1 pm
	2 pm
	3 pm
	4 pm
	5 pm
	6 pm
	7 pm
	8 pm
	9 pm

Date:

SCRIPTURE – DRAW CLOSER TO THE KING OF KINGS: Use your name in the place of a character in the scripture you're reading; imagine yourself in that time, using all 5 senses. Pray scripture back to God. Write the scripture down, read it, repeat it out loud throughout the day, memorize it, and meditate on it.

WORSHIP – PRAISE HIM FOR WHO HE IS: How will you glorify and magnify Him today? There is no room here for making personal petitions.

PURE HEART – ASK HIM TO PURIFY YOUR MIND AND HEART: Replace negative thoughts with higher thoughts. God's thoughts are noble, pure, lovely, excellent, right, true, and admirable. Ask God to reveal areas in your life that grieve the Holy Spirit. Confess with a contrite heart and receive forgiveness. As you confess, turn your palms up and release your sin, worry, and anxiety over to God. Now turn your palms down and receive God's love, mercy, favor, and grace.

THANKFULNESS – NAME THOSE THINGS YOU ARE THANKFUL FOR: There's always something to be grateful for. Name them one by one and come back often to rekindle the joy of each one of them.

O

O

O

O

O

O

O

REFLECTION & REVELATION – PRACTICE LISTENING FOR GOD: God promises that if you draw near to Him, He will tell you things you do not know. Who does God bring to mind? Where is God leading you? Reflect on God's perspective.	TASKS
PRAYER – YOU HAVE NOT BECAUSE YOU ASK NOT: Pray for family, friends, relationships, unity, community, world, church, favor, wisdom, God's will, work, and your future. Pray about anything and everything, without ceasing.	
OBEDIENCE – STAND, SHARE, SERVE: Take steps of faith, and obey promptly. The level of miracles in your life will be directly related to your level of obedience. Faith without works is dead. You have an assignment, a destiny to fulfill.	
	6 am
	7 am
	8 am
	9 am
	10 am
	11 am
	12 pm
	1 pm
	2 pm
	3 pm
	4 pm
	5 pm
	6 pm
	7 pm
	8 pm
	9 pm

Date:

SCRIPTURE – DRAW CLOSER TO THE KING OF KINGS: Use your name in the place of a character in the scripture you're reading; imagine yourself in that time, using all 5 senses. Pray scripture back to God. Write the scripture down, read it, repeat it out loud throughout the day, memorize it, and meditate on it.

WORSHIP – PRAISE HIM FOR WHO HE IS: How will you glorify and magnify Him today? There is no room here for making personal petitions.

PURE HEART – ASK HIM TO PURIFY YOUR MIND AND HEART: Replace negative thoughts with higher thoughts. God's thoughts are noble, pure, lovely, excellent, right, true, and admirable. Ask God to reveal areas in your life that grieve the Holy Spirit. Confess with a contrite heart and receive forgiveness. As you confess, turn your palms up and release your sin, worry, and anxiety over to God. Now turn your palms down and receive God's love, mercy, favor, and grace.

THANKFULNESS – NAME THOSE THINGS YOU ARE THANKFUL FOR: There's always something to be grateful for. Name them one by one and come back often to rekindle the joy of each one of them.

O

O

O

O

O

O

O

REFLECTION & REVELATION – PRACTICE LISTENING FOR GOD: God promises that if you draw near to Him, He will tell you things you do not know. Who does God bring to mind? Where is God leading you? Reflect on God's perspective.	TASKS
PRAYER – YOU HAVE NOT BECAUSE YOU ASK NOT: Pray for family, friends, relationships, unity, community, world, church, favor, wisdom, God's will, work, and your future. Pray about anything and everything, without ceasing.	
OBEDIENCE – STAND, SHARE, SERVE: Take steps of faith, and obey promptly. The level of miracles in your life will be directly related to your level of obedience. Faith without works is dead. You have an assignment, a destiny to fulfill.	
	6 am
	7 am
	8 am
	9 am
	10 am
	11 am
	12 pm
	1 pm
	2 pm
	3 pm
	4 pm
	5 pm
	6 pm
	7 pm
	8 pm
	9 pm

Date:

SCRIPTURE – DRAW CLOSER TO THE KING OF KINGS: Use your name in the place of a character in the scripture you're reading; imagine yourself in that time, using all 5 senses. Pray scripture back to God. Write the scripture down, read it, repeat it out loud throughout the day, memorize it, and meditate on it.

WORSHIP – PRAISE HIM FOR WHO HE IS: How will you glorify and magnify Him today? There is no room here for making personal petitions.

PURE HEART – ASK HIM TO PURIFY YOUR MIND AND HEART: Replace negative thoughts with higher thoughts. God's thoughts are noble, pure, lovely, excellent, right, true, and admirable. Ask God to reveal areas in your life that grieve the Holy Spirit. Confess with a contrite heart and receive forgiveness. As you confess, turn your palms up and release your sin, worry, and anxiety over to God. Now turn your palms down and receive God's love, mercy, favor, and grace.

THANKFULNESS – NAME THOSE THINGS YOU ARE THANKFUL FOR: There's always something to be grateful for. Name them one by one and come back often to rekindle the joy of each one of them.

O

O

O

O

O

O

O

	TASKS
REFLECTION & REVELATION – PRACTICE LISTENING FOR GOD: God promises that if you draw near to Him, He will tell you things you do not know. Who does God bring to mind? Where is God leading you? Reflect on God's perspective.	
PRAYER – YOU HAVE NOT BECAUSE YOU ASK NOT: Pray for family, friends, relationships, unity, community, world, church, favor, wisdom, God's will, work, and your future. Pray about anything and everything, without ceasing.	
OBEDIENCE – STAND, SHARE, SERVE: Take steps of faith, and obey promptly. The level of miracles in your life will be directly related to your level of obedience. Faith without works is dead. You have an assignment, a destiny to fulfill.	
	6 am
	7 am
	8 am
	9 am
	10 am
	11 am
	12 pm
	1 pm
	2 pm
	3 pm
	4 pm
	5 pm
	6 pm
	7 pm
	8 pm
	9 pm

Date:

SCRIPTURE – DRAW CLOSER TO THE KING OF KINGS: Use your name in the place of a character in the scripture you're reading; imagine yourself in that time, using all 5 senses. Pray scripture back to God. Write the scripture down, read it, repeat it out loud throughout the day, memorize it, and meditate on it.

WORSHIP – PRAISE HIM FOR WHO HE IS: How will you glorify and magnify Him today? There is no room here for making personal petitions.

PURE HEART – ASK HIM TO PURIFY YOUR MIND AND HEART: Replace negative thoughts with higher thoughts. God's thoughts are noble, pure, lovely, excellent, right, true, and admirable. Ask God to reveal areas in your life that grieve the Holy Spirit. Confess with a contrite heart and receive forgiveness. As you confess, turn your palms up and release your sin, worry, and anxiety over to God. Now turn your palms down and receive God's love, mercy, favor, and grace.

THANKFULNESS – NAME THOSE THINGS YOU ARE THANKFUL FOR: There's always something to be grateful for. Name them one by one and come back often to rekindle the joy of each one of them.

O

O

O

O

O

O

O

	TASKS
REFLECTION & REVELATION – PRACTICE LISTENING FOR GOD: God promises that if you draw near to Him, He will tell you things you do not know. Who does God bring to mind? Where is God leading you? Reflect on God's perspective.	
PRAYER – YOU HAVE NOT BECAUSE YOU ASK NOT: Pray for family, friends, relationships, unity, community, world, church, favor, wisdom, God's will, work, and your future. Pray about anything and everything, without ceasing.	
OBEDIENCE – STAND, SHARE, SERVE: Take steps of faith, and obey promptly. The level of miracles in your life will be directly related to your level of obedience. Faith without works is dead. You have an assignment, a destiny to fulfill.	
	6 am
	7 am
	8 am
	9 am
	10 am
	11 am
	12 pm
	1 pm
	2 pm
	3 pm
	4 pm
	5 pm
	6 pm
	7 pm
	8 pm
	9 pm

WEEKLY FOCUS

Last Week's Reflection
Areas to Celebrate:
Areas to Improve:
What did I learn

This Week's Planning
Plan for joyful occasions. Joy is your strength, refreshment, energy, and beauty. What are you looking forward to this week? Find something to laugh about and share it.

Projects/Areas of focus this week:

- [ ]
- [ ]
- [ ]
- [ ]
- [ ]
- [ ]
- [ ]

AREAS TO SIMPLIFY – where to set godly boundaries

	What is important	What is not important	Why	What are Facts/Feelings	Benefits of continuing/not continuing	Pray about possibilities and solutions
Time						
Energy						
Money						
Relationships						
Possessions						

FASTING: Take authority over what controls me; lean on God; keep Christ-focused
What to fast:
Time to fast:
How to fast:
Check motives:

ADDITIONAL REFLECTION

Date:

SCRIPTURE – DRAW CLOSER TO THE KING OF KINGS: Use your name in the place of a character in the scripture you're reading; imagine yourself in that time, using all 5 senses. Pray scripture back to God. Write the scripture down, read it, repeat it out loud throughout the day, memorize it, and meditate on it.

WORSHIP – PRAISE HIM FOR WHO HE IS: How will you glorify and magnify Him today? There is no room here for making personal petitions.

PURE HEART – ASK HIM TO PURIFY YOUR MIND AND HEART: Replace negative thoughts with higher thoughts. God's thoughts are noble, pure, lovely, excellent, right, true, and admirable. Ask God to reveal areas in your life that grieve the Holy Spirit. Confess with a contrite heart and receive forgiveness. As you confess, turn your palms up and release your sin, worry, and anxiety over to God. Now turn your palms down and receive God's love, mercy, favor, and grace.

THANKFULNESS – NAME THOSE THINGS YOU ARE THANKFUL FOR: There's always something to be grateful for. Name them one by one and come back often to rekindle the joy of each one of them.

O

O

O

O

O

O

O

REFLECTION & REVELATION – PRACTICE LISTENING FOR GOD: God promises that if you draw near to Him, He will tell you things you do not know. Who does God bring to mind? Where is God leading you? Reflect on God's perspective.	TASKS
PRAYER – YOU HAVE NOT BECAUSE YOU ASK NOT: Pray for family, friends, relationships, unity, community, world, church, favor, wisdom, God's will, work, and your future. Pray about anything and everything, without ceasing.	
OBEDIENCE – STAND, SHARE, SERVE: Take steps of faith, and obey promptly. The level of miracles in your life will be directly related to your level of obedience. Faith without works is dead. You have an assignment, a destiny to fulfill.	
	6 am
	7 am
	8 am
	9 am
	10 am
	11 am
	12 pm
	1 pm
	2 pm
	3 pm
	4 pm
	5 pm
	6 pm
	7 pm
	8 pm
	9 pm

Date:

SCRIPTURE – DRAW CLOSER TO THE KING OF KINGS: Use your name in the place of a character in the scripture you're reading; imagine yourself in that time, using all 5 senses. Pray scripture back to God. Write the scripture down, read it, repeat it out loud throughout the day, memorize it, and meditate on it.

WORSHIP – PRAISE HIM FOR WHO HE IS: How will you glorify and magnify Him today? There is no room here for making personal petitions.

PURE HEART – ASK HIM TO PURIFY YOUR MIND AND HEART: Replace negative thoughts with higher thoughts. God's thoughts are noble, pure, lovely, excellent, right, true, and admirable. Ask God to reveal areas in your life that grieve the Holy Spirit. Confess with a contrite heart and receive forgiveness. As you confess, turn your palms up and release your sin, worry, and anxiety over to God. Now turn your palms down and receive God's love, mercy, favor, and grace.

THANKFULNESS – NAME THOSE THINGS YOU ARE THANKFUL FOR: There's always something to be grateful for. Name them one by one and come back often to rekindle the joy of each one of them.

O

O

O

O

O

O

O

O

	TASKS
REFLECTION & REVELATION – PRACTICE LISTENING FOR GOD: God promises that if you draw near to Him, He will tell you things you do not know. Who does God bring to mind? Where is God leading you? Reflect on God's perspective.	
PRAYER – YOU HAVE NOT BECAUSE YOU ASK NOT: Pray for family, friends, relationships, unity, community, world, church, favor, wisdom, God's will, work, and your future. Pray about anything and everything, without ceasing.	
OBEDIENCE – STAND, SHARE, SERVE: Take steps of faith, and obey promptly. The level of miracles in your life will be directly related to your level of obedience. Faith without works is dead. You have an assignment, a destiny to fulfill.	
	6 am
	7 am
	8 am
	9 am
	10 am
	11 am
	12 pm
	1 pm
	2 pm
	3 pm
	4 pm
	5 pm
	6 pm
	7 pm
	8 pm
	9 pm

Date:

SCRIPTURE – DRAW CLOSER TO THE KING OF KINGS: Use your name in the place of a character in the scripture you're reading; imagine yourself in that time, using all 5 senses. Pray scripture back to God. Write the scripture down, read it, repeat it out loud throughout the day, memorize it, and meditate on it.

_____
_____
_____
_____
_____
_____
_____
_____
_____
_____
_____
_____
_____

WORSHIP – PRAISE HIM FOR WHO HE IS: How will you glorify and magnify Him today? There is no room here for making personal petitions.

_____
_____
_____
_____

PURE HEART – ASK HIM TO PURIFY YOUR MIND AND HEART: Replace negative thoughts with higher thoughts. God's thoughts are noble, pure, lovely, excellent, right, true, and admirable. Ask God to reveal areas in your life that grieve the Holy Spirit. Confess with a contrite heart and receive forgiveness. As you confess, turn your palms up and release your sin, worry, and anxiety over to God. Now turn your palms down and receive God's love, mercy, favor, and grace.

_____
_____
_____

THANKFULNESS – NAME THOSE THINGS YOU ARE THANKFUL FOR: There's always something to be grateful for. Name them one by one and come back often to rekindle the joy of each one of them.

O _____
O _____
O _____
O _____
O _____
O _____
O _____

REFLECTION & REVELATION – PRACTICE LISTENING FOR GOD: God promises that if you draw near to Him, He will tell you things you do not know. Who does God bring to mind? Where is God leading you? Reflect on God's perspective.	TASKS
PRAYER – YOU HAVE NOT BECAUSE YOU ASK NOT: Pray for family, friends, relationships, unity, community, world, church, favor, wisdom, God's will, work, and your future. Pray about anything and everything, without ceasing.	
OBEDIENCE – STAND, SHARE, SERVE: Take steps of faith, and obey promptly. The level of miracles in your life will be directly related to your level of obedience. Faith without works is dead. You have an assignment, a destiny to fulfill.	
	6 am
	7 am
	8 am
	9 am
	10 am
	11 am
	12 pm
	1 pm
	2 pm
	3 pm
	4 pm
	5 pm
	6 pm
	7 pm
	8 pm
	9 pm

Date:

SCRIPTURE – DRAW CLOSER TO THE KING OF KINGS: Use your name in the place of a character in the scripture you're reading; imagine yourself in that time, using all 5 senses. Pray scripture back to God. Write the scripture down, read it, repeat it out loud throughout the day, memorize it, and meditate on it.

WORSHIP – PRAISE HIM FOR WHO HE IS: How will you glorify and magnify Him today? There is no room here for making personal petitions.

PURE HEART – ASK HIM TO PURIFY YOUR MIND AND HEART: Replace negative thoughts with higher thoughts. God's thoughts are noble, pure, lovely, excellent, right, true, and admirable. Ask God to reveal areas in your life that grieve the Holy Spirit. Confess with a contrite heart and receive forgiveness. As you confess, turn your palms up and release your sin, worry, and anxiety over to God. Now turn your palms down and receive God's love, mercy, favor, and grace.

THANKFULNESS – NAME THOSE THINGS YOU ARE THANKFUL FOR: There's always something to be grateful for. Name them one by one and come back often to rekindle the joy of each one of them.

O

O

O

O

O

O

O

	TASKS
REFLECTION & REVELATION – PRACTICE LISTENING FOR GOD: God promises that if you draw near to Him, He will tell you things you do not know. Who does God bring to mind? Where is God leading you? Reflect on God's perspective.	
PRAYER – YOU HAVE NOT BECAUSE YOU ASK NOT: Pray for family, friends, relationships, unity, community, world, church, favor, wisdom, God's will, work, and your future. Pray about anything and everything, without ceasing.	
OBEDIENCE – STAND, SHARE, SERVE: Take steps of faith, and obey promptly. The level of miracles in your life will be directly related to your level of obedience. Faith without works is dead. You have an assignment, a destiny to fulfill.	
	6 am
	7 am
	8 am
	9 am
	10 am
	11 am
	12 pm
	1 pm
	2 pm
	3 pm
	4 pm
	5 pm
	6 pm
	7 pm
	8 pm
	9 pm

Date:

SCRIPTURE – DRAW CLOSER TO THE KING OF KINGS: Use your name in the place of a character in the scripture you're reading; imagine yourself in that time, using all 5 senses. Pray scripture back to God. Write the scripture down, read it, repeat it out loud throughout the day, memorize it, and meditate on it.

_____
_____
_____
_____
_____
_____
_____
_____
_____
_____
_____
_____

WORSHIP – PRAISE HIM FOR WHO HE IS: How will you glorify and magnify Him today? There is no room here for making personal petitions.

_____
_____
_____
_____

PURE HEART – ASK HIM TO PURIFY YOUR MIND AND HEART: Replace negative thoughts with higher thoughts. God's thoughts are noble, pure, lovely, excellent, right, true, and admirable. Ask God to reveal areas in your life that grieve the Holy Spirit. Confess with a contrite heart and receive forgiveness. As you confess, turn your palms up and release your sin, worry, and anxiety over to God. Now turn your palms down and receive God's love, mercy, favor, and grace.

_____
_____
_____

THANKFULNESS – NAME THOSE THINGS YOU ARE THANKFUL FOR: There's always something to be grateful for. Name them one by one and come back often to rekindle the joy of each one of them.

O
O
O
O
O
O
O

	TASKS
REFLECTION & REVELATION – PRACTICE LISTENING FOR GOD: God promises that if you draw near to Him, He will tell you things you do not know. Who does God bring to mind? Where is God leading you? Reflect on God's perspective.	
PRAYER – YOU HAVE NOT BECAUSE YOU ASK NOT: Pray for family, friends, relationships, unity, community, world, church, favor, wisdom, God's will, work, and your future. Pray about anything and everything, without ceasing.	
OBEDIENCE – STAND, SHARE, SERVE: Take steps of faith, and obey promptly. The level of miracles in your life will be directly related to your level of obedience. Faith without works is dead. You have an assignment, a destiny to fulfill.	
	6 am
	7 am
	8 am
	9 am
	10 am
	11 am
	12 pm
	1 pm
	2 pm
	3 pm
	4 pm
	5 pm
	6 pm
	7 pm
	8 pm
	9 pm

Date:

SCRIPTURE – DRAW CLOSER TO THE KING OF KINGS: Use your name in the place of a character in the scripture you're reading; imagine yourself in that time, using all 5 senses. Pray scripture back to God. Write the scripture down, read it, repeat it out loud throughout the day, memorize it, and meditate on it.

_____

_____

_____

_____

_____

_____

_____

_____

_____

_____

_____

_____

_____

WORSHIP – PRAISE HIM FOR WHO HE IS: How will you glorify and magnify Him today? There is no room here for making personal petitions.

_____

_____

_____

PURE HEART – ASK HIM TO PURIFY YOUR MIND AND HEART: Replace negative thoughts with higher thoughts. God's thoughts are noble, pure, lovely, excellent, right, true, and admirable. Ask God to reveal areas in your life that grieve the Holy Spirit. Confess with a contrite heart and receive forgiveness. As you confess, turn your palms up and release your sin, worry, and anxiety over to God. Now turn your palms down and receive God's love, mercy, favor, and grace.

_____

_____

_____

THANKFULNESS – NAME THOSE THINGS YOU ARE THANKFUL FOR: There's always something to be grateful for. Name them one by one and come back often to rekindle the joy of each one of them.

O

O

O

O

O

O

O

	TASKS
REFLECTION & REVELATION – PRACTICE LISTENING FOR GOD: God promises that if you draw near to Him, He will tell you things you do not know. Who does God bring to mind? Where is God leading you? Reflect on God's perspective.	
PRAYER – YOU HAVE NOT BECAUSE YOU ASK NOT: Pray for family, friends, relationships, unity, community, world, church, favor, wisdom, God's will, work, and your future. Pray about anything and everything, without ceasing.	
OBEDIENCE – STAND, SHARE, SERVE: Take steps of faith, and obey promptly. The level of miracles in your life will be directly related to your level of obedience. Faith without works is dead. You have an assignment, a destiny to fulfill.	
	6 am
	7 am
	8 am
	9 am
	10 am
	11 am
	12 pm
	1 pm
	2 pm
	3 pm
	4 pm
	5 pm
	6 pm
	7 pm
	8 pm
	9 pm

Date:

SCRIPTURE – DRAW CLOSER TO THE KING OF KINGS: Use your name in the place of a character in the scripture you're reading; imagine yourself in that time, using all 5 senses. Pray scripture back to God. Write the scripture down, read it, repeat it out loud throughout the day, memorize it, and meditate on it.

WORSHIP – PRAISE HIM FOR WHO HE IS: How will you glorify and magnify Him today? There is no room here for making personal petitions.

PURE HEART – ASK HIM TO PURIFY YOUR MIND AND HEART: Replace negative thoughts with higher thoughts. God's thoughts are noble, pure, lovely, excellent, right, true, and admirable. Ask God to reveal areas in your life that grieve the Holy Spirit. Confess with a contrite heart and receive forgiveness. As you confess, turn your palms up and release your sin, worry, and anxiety over to God. Now turn your palms down and receive God's love, mercy, favor, and grace.

THANKFULNESS – NAME THOSE THINGS YOU ARE THANKFUL FOR: There's always something to be grateful for. Name them one by one and come back often to rekindle the joy of each one of them.

O

O

O

O

O

O

O

	TASKS
REFLECTION & REVELATION – PRACTICE LISTENING FOR GOD: God promises that if you draw near to Him, He will tell you things you do not know. Who does God bring to mind? Where is God leading you? Reflect on God's perspective.	
PRAYER – YOU HAVE NOT BECAUSE YOU ASK NOT: Pray for family, friends, relationships, unity, community, world, church, favor, wisdom, God's will, work, and your future. Pray about anything and everything, without ceasing.	
OBEDIENCE – STAND, SHARE, SERVE: Take steps of faith, and obey promptly. The level of miracles in your life will be directly related to your level of obedience. Faith without works is dead. You have an assignment, a destiny to fulfill.	
	6 am
	7 am
	8 am
	9 am
	10 am
	11 am
	12 pm
	1 pm
	2 pm
	3 pm
	4 pm
	5 pm
	6 pm
	7 pm
	8 pm
	9 pm

WEEKLY FOCUS

Last Week's Reflection
Areas to Celebrate:
Areas to Improve:
What did I learn

This Week's Planning
Plan for joyful occasions. Joy is your strength, refreshment, energy, and beauty. What are you looking forward to this week? Find something to laugh about and share it.

Projects/Areas of focus this week:

- ☐
- ☐
- ☐
- ☐
- ☐
- ☐
- ☐

AREAS TO SIMPLIFY – where to set godly boundaries

	What is important	What is not important	Why	What are Facts/Feelings	Benefits of continuing/not continuing	Pray about possibilities and solutions
Time						
Energy						
Money						
Relationships						
Possessions						

FASTING: Take authority over what controls me; lean on God; keep Christ-focused
What to fast:
Time to fast:
How to fast:
Check motives:

ADDITIONAL REFLECTION

Date:

SCRIPTURE – DRAW CLOSER TO THE KING OF KINGS: Use your name in the place of a character in the scripture you're reading; imagine yourself in that time, using all 5 senses. Pray scripture back to God. Write the scripture down, read it, repeat it out loud throughout the day, memorize it, and meditate on it.

WORSHIP – PRAISE HIM FOR WHO HE IS: How will you glorify and magnify Him today? There is no room here for making personal petitions.

PURE HEART – ASK HIM TO PURIFY YOUR MIND AND HEART: Replace negative thoughts with higher thoughts. God's thoughts are noble, pure, lovely, excellent, right, true, and admirable. Ask God to reveal areas in your life that grieve the Holy Spirit. Confess with a contrite heart and receive forgiveness. As you confess, turn your palms up and release your sin, worry, and anxiety over to God. Now turn your palms down and receive God's love, mercy, favor, and grace.

THANKFULNESS – NAME THOSE THINGS YOU ARE THANKFUL FOR: There's always something to be grateful for. Name them one by one and come back often to rekindle the joy of each one of them.

O

O

O

O

O

O

O

REFLECTION & REVELATION – PRACTICE LISTENING FOR GOD: God promises that if you draw near to Him, He will tell you things you do not know. Who does God bring to mind? Where is God leading you? Reflect on God's perspective.	TASKS
PRAYER – YOU HAVE NOT BECAUSE YOU ASK NOT: Pray for family, friends, relationships, unity, community, world, church, favor, wisdom, God's will, work, and your future. Pray about anything and everything, without ceasing.	
OBEDIENCE – STAND, SHARE, SERVE: Take steps of faith, and obey promptly. The level of miracles in your life will be directly related to your level of obedience. Faith without works is dead. You have an assignment, a destiny to fulfill.	
	6 am
	7 am
	8 am
	9 am
	10 am
	11 am
	12 pm
	1 pm
	2 pm
	3 pm
	4 pm
	5 pm
	6 pm
	7 pm
	8 pm
	9 pm

Date:

SCRIPTURE – DRAW CLOSER TO THE KING OF KINGS: Use your name in the place of a character in the scripture you're reading; imagine yourself in that time, using all 5 senses. Pray scripture back to God. Write the scripture down, read it, repeat it out loud throughout the day, memorize it, and meditate on it.

WORSHIP – PRAISE HIM FOR WHO HE IS: How will you glorify and magnify Him today? There is no room here for making personal petitions.

PURE HEART – ASK HIM TO PURIFY YOUR MIND AND HEART: Replace negative thoughts with higher thoughts. God's thoughts are noble, pure, lovely, excellent, right, true, and admirable. Ask God to reveal areas in your life that grieve the Holy Spirit. Confess with a contrite heart and receive forgiveness. As you confess, turn your palms up and release your sin, worry, and anxiety over to God. Now turn your palms down and receive God's love, mercy, favor, and grace.

THANKFULNESS – NAME THOSE THINGS YOU ARE THANKFUL FOR: There's always something to be grateful for. Name them one by one and come back often to rekindle the joy of each one of them.

O

O

O

O

O

O

O

REFLECTION & REVELATION – PRACTICE LISTENING FOR GOD: God promises that if you draw near to Him, He will tell you things you do not know. Who does God bring to mind? Where is God leading you? Reflect on God's perspective.	TASKS
PRAYER – YOU HAVE NOT BECAUSE YOU ASK NOT: Pray for family, friends, relationships, unity, community, world, church, favor, wisdom, God's will, work, and your future. Pray about anything and everything, without ceasing.	
OBEDIENCE – STAND, SHARE, SERVE: Take steps of faith, and obey promptly. The level of miracles in your life will be directly related to your level of obedience. Faith without works is dead. You have an assignment, a destiny to fulfill.	
	6 am
	7 am
	8 am
	9 am
	10 am
	11 am
	12 pm
	1 pm
	2 pm
	3 pm
	4 pm
	5 pm
	6 pm
	7 pm
	8 pm
	9 pm

Date:

SCRIPTURE – DRAW CLOSER TO THE KING OF KINGS: Use your name in the place of a character in the scripture you're reading; imagine yourself in that time, using all 5 senses. Pray scripture back to God. Write the scripture down, read it, repeat it out loud throughout the day, memorize it, and meditate on it.

WORSHIP – PRAISE HIM FOR WHO HE IS: How will you glorify and magnify Him today? There is no room here for making personal petitions.

PURE HEART – ASK HIM TO PURIFY YOUR MIND AND HEART: Replace negative thoughts with higher thoughts. God's thoughts are noble, pure, lovely, excellent, right, true, and admirable. Ask God to reveal areas in your life that grieve the Holy Spirit. Confess with a contrite heart and receive forgiveness. As you confess, turn your palms up and release your sin, worry, and anxiety over to God. Now turn your palms down and receive God's love, mercy, favor, and grace.

THANKFULNESS – NAME THOSE THINGS YOU ARE THANKFUL FOR: There's always something to be grateful for. Name them one by one and come back often to rekindle the joy of each one of them.

O

O

O

O

O

O

O

REFLECTION & REVELATION – PRACTICE LISTENING FOR GOD: God promises that if you draw near to Him, He will tell you things you do not know. Who does God bring to mind? Where is God leading you? Reflect on God's perspective.	TASKS
PRAYER – YOU HAVE NOT BECAUSE YOU ASK NOT: Pray for family, friends, relationships, unity, community, world, church, favor, wisdom, God's will, work, and your future. Pray about anything and everything, without ceasing.	
OBEDIENCE – STAND, SHARE, SERVE: Take steps of faith, and obey promptly. The level of miracles in your life will be directly related to your level of obedience. Faith without works is dead. You have an assignment, a destiny to fulfill.	
	6 am
	7 am
	8 am
	9 am
	10 am
	11 am
	12 pm
	1 pm
	2 pm
	3 pm
	4 pm
	5 pm
	6 pm
	7 pm
	8 pm
	9 pm

Date:

SCRIPTURE – DRAW CLOSER TO THE KING OF KINGS: Use your name in the place of a character in the scripture you're reading; imagine yourself in that time, using all 5 senses. Pray scripture back to God. Write the scripture down, read it, repeat it out loud throughout the day, memorize it, and meditate on it.

WORSHIP – PRAISE HIM FOR WHO HE IS: How will you glorify and magnify Him today? There is no room here for making personal petitions.

PURE HEART – ASK HIM TO PURIFY YOUR MIND AND HEART: Replace negative thoughts with higher thoughts. God's thoughts are noble, pure, lovely, excellent, right, true, and admirable. Ask God to reveal areas in your life that grieve the Holy Spirit. Confess with a contrite heart and receive forgiveness. As you confess, turn your palms up and release your sin, worry, and anxiety over to God. Now turn your palms down and receive God's love, mercy, favor, and grace.

THANKFULNESS – NAME THOSE THINGS YOU ARE THANKFUL FOR: There's always something to be grateful for. Name them one by one and come back often to rekindle the joy of each one of them.

O

O

O

O

O

O

O

REFLECTION & REVELATION – PRACTICE LISTENING FOR GOD: God promises that if you draw near to Him, He will tell you things you do not know. Who does God bring to mind? Where is God leading you? Reflect on God's perspective.	TASKS
PRAYER – YOU HAVE NOT BECAUSE YOU ASK NOT: Pray for family, friends, relationships, unity, community, world, church, favor, wisdom, God's will, work, and your future. Pray about anything and everything, without ceasing.	
OBEDIENCE – STAND, SHARE, SERVE: Take steps of faith, and obey promptly. The level of miracles in your life will be directly related to your level of obedience. Faith without works is dead. You have an assignment, a destiny to fulfill.	
	6 am
	7 am
	8 am
	9 am
	10 am
	11 am
	12 pm
	1 pm
	2 pm
	3 pm
	4 pm
	5 pm
	6 pm
	7 pm
	8 pm
	9 pm

Date:

SCRIPTURE – DRAW CLOSER TO THE KING OF KINGS: Use your name in the place of a character in the scripture you're reading; imagine yourself in that time, using all 5 senses. Pray scripture back to God. Write the scripture down, read it, repeat it out loud throughout the day, memorize it, and meditate on it.

WORSHIP – PRAISE HIM FOR WHO HE IS: How will you glorify and magnify Him today? There is no room here for making personal petitions.

PURE HEART – ASK HIM TO PURIFY YOUR MIND AND HEART: Replace negative thoughts with higher thoughts. God's thoughts are noble, pure, lovely, excellent, right, true, and admirable. Ask God to reveal areas in your life that grieve the Holy Spirit. Confess with a contrite heart and receive forgiveness. As you confess, turn your palms up and release your sin, worry, and anxiety over to God. Now turn your palms down and receive God's love, mercy, favor, and grace.

THANKFULNESS – NAME THOSE THINGS YOU ARE THANKFUL FOR: There's always something to be grateful for. Name them one by one and come back often to rekindle the joy of each one of them.

O

O

O

O

O

O

O

REFLECTION & REVELATION – PRACTICE LISTENING FOR GOD: God promises that if you draw near to Him, He will tell you things you do not know. Who does God bring to mind? Where is God leading you? Reflect on God's perspective.	TASKS
PRAYER – YOU HAVE NOT BECAUSE YOU ASK NOT: Pray for family, friends, relationships, unity, community, world, church, favor, wisdom, God's will, work, and your future. Pray about anything and everything, without ceasing.	
OBEDIENCE – STAND, SHARE, SERVE: Take steps of faith, and obey promptly. The level of miracles in your life will be directly related to your level of obedience. Faith without works is dead. You have an assignment, a destiny to fulfill.	
	6 am
	7 am
	8 am
	9 am
	10 am
	11 am
	12 pm
	1 pm
	2 pm
	3 pm
	4 pm
	5 pm
	6 pm
	7 pm
	8 pm
	9 pm

Date:

SCRIPTURE – DRAW CLOSER TO THE KING OF KINGS: Use your name in the place of a character in the scripture you're reading; imagine yourself in that time, using all 5 senses. Pray scripture back to God. Write the scripture down, read it, repeat it out loud throughout the day, memorize it, and meditate on it.

WORSHIP – PRAISE HIM FOR WHO HE IS: How will you glorify and magnify Him today? There is no room here for making personal petitions.

PURE HEART – ASK HIM TO PURIFY YOUR MIND AND HEART: Replace negative thoughts with higher thoughts. God's thoughts are noble, pure, lovely, excellent, right, true, and admirable. Ask God to reveal areas in your life that grieve the Holy Spirit. Confess with a contrite heart and receive forgiveness. As you confess, turn your palms up and release your sin, worry, and anxiety over to God. Now turn your palms down and receive God's love, mercy, favor, and grace.

THANKFULNESS – NAME THOSE THINGS YOU ARE THANKFUL FOR: There's always something to be grateful for. Name them one by one and come back often to rekindle the joy of each one of them.

O

O

O

O

O

O

O

REFLECTION & REVELATION – PRACTICE LISTENING FOR GOD: God promises that if you draw near to Him, He will tell you things you do not know. Who does God bring to mind? Where is God leading you? Reflect on God's perspective.	TASKS
PRAYER – YOU HAVE NOT BECAUSE YOU ASK NOT: Pray for family, friends, relationships, unity, community, world, church, favor, wisdom, God's will, work, and your future. Pray about anything and everything, without ceasing.	
OBEDIENCE – STAND, SHARE, SERVE: Take steps of faith, and obey promptly. The level of miracles in your life will be directly related to your level of obedience. Faith without works is dead. You have an assignment, a destiny to fulfill.	
	6 am
	7 am
	8 am
	9 am
	10 am
	11 am
	12 pm
	1 pm
	2 pm
	3 pm
	4 pm
	5 pm
	6 pm
	7 pm
	8 pm
	9 pm

Date:

SCRIPTURE – DRAW CLOSER TO THE KING OF KINGS: Use your name in the place of a character in the scripture you're reading; imagine yourself in that time, using all 5 senses. Pray scripture back to God. Write the scripture down, read it, repeat it out loud throughout the day, memorize it, and meditate on it.

WORSHIP – PRAISE HIM FOR WHO HE IS: How will you glorify and magnify Him today? There is no room here for making personal petitions.

PURE HEART – ASK HIM TO PURIFY YOUR MIND AND HEART: Replace negative thoughts with higher thoughts. God's thoughts are noble, pure, lovely, excellent, right, true, and admirable. Ask God to reveal areas in your life that grieve the Holy Spirit. Confess with a contrite heart and receive forgiveness. As you confess, turn your palms up and release your sin, worry, and anxiety over to God. Now turn your palms down and receive God's love, mercy, favor, and grace.

THANKFULNESS – NAME THOSE THINGS YOU ARE THANKFUL FOR: There's always something to be grateful for. Name them one by one and come back often to rekindle the joy of each one of them.

O

O

O

O

O

O

O

REFLECTION & REVELATION – PRACTICE LISTENING FOR GOD: God promises that if you draw near to Him, He will tell you things you do not know. Who does God bring to mind? Where is God leading you? Reflect on God's perspective.	TASKS
PRAYER – YOU HAVE NOT BECAUSE YOU ASK NOT: Pray for family, friends, relationships, unity, community, world, church, favor, wisdom, God's will, work, and your future. Pray about anything and everything, without ceasing.	
OBEDIENCE – STAND, SHARE, SERVE: Take steps of faith, and obey promptly. The level of miracles in your life will be directly related to your level of obedience. Faith without works is dead. You have an assignment, a destiny to fulfill.	
	6 am
	7 am
	8 am
	9 am
	10 am
	11 am
	12 pm
	1 pm
	2 pm
	3 pm
	4 pm
	5 pm
	6 pm
	7 pm
	8 pm
	9 pm

WEEKLY FOCUS

Last Week's Reflection
Areas to Celebrate:
Areas to Improve:
What did I learn

This Week's Planning
Plan for joyful occasions. Joy is your strength, refreshment, energy, and beauty. What are you looking forward to this week? Find something to laugh about and share it.

Projects/Areas of focus this week:

- [ ]
- [ ]
- [ ]
- [ ]
- [ ]
- [ ]
- [ ]

AREAS TO SIMPLIFY – where to set godly boundaries

	What is important	What is not important	Why	What are Facts/Feelings	Benefits of continuing/not continuing	Pray about possibilities and solutions
Time						
Energy						
Money						
Relationships						
Possessions						

FASTING: Take authority over what controls me; lean on God; keep Christ-focused
What to fast:
Time to fast:
How to fast:
Check motives:

ADDITIONAL REFLECTION

Date:

SCRIPTURE – DRAW CLOSER TO THE KING OF KINGS: Use your name in the place of a character in the scripture you're reading; imagine yourself in that time, using all 5 senses. Pray scripture back to God. Write the scripture down, read it, repeat it out loud throughout the day, memorize it, and meditate on it.

WORSHIP – PRAISE HIM FOR WHO HE IS: How will you glorify and magnify Him today? There is no room here for making personal petitions.

PURE HEART – ASK HIM TO PURIFY YOUR MIND AND HEART: Replace negative thoughts with higher thoughts. God's thoughts are noble, pure, lovely, excellent, right, true, and admirable. Ask God to reveal areas in your life that grieve the Holy Spirit. Confess with a contrite heart and receive forgiveness. As you confess, turn your palms up and release your sin, worry, and anxiety over to God. Now turn your palms down and receive God's love, mercy, favor, and grace.

THANKFULNESS – NAME THOSE THINGS YOU ARE THANKFUL FOR: There's always something to be grateful for. Name them one by one and come back often to rekindle the joy of each one of them.

O

O

O

O

O

O

O

REFLECTION & REVELATION – PRACTICE LISTENING FOR GOD: God promises that if you draw near to Him, He will tell you things you do not know. Who does God bring to mind? Where is God leading you? Reflect on God's perspective.	TASKS
PRAYER – YOU HAVE NOT BECAUSE YOU ASK NOT: Pray for family, friends, relationships, unity, community, world, church, favor, wisdom, God's will, work, and your future. Pray about anything and everything, without ceasing.	
OBEDIENCE – STAND, SHARE, SERVE: Take steps of faith, and obey promptly. The level of miracles in your life will be directly related to your level of obedience. Faith without works is dead. You have an assignment, a destiny to fulfill.	
	6 am
	7 am
	8 am
	9 am
	10 am
	11 am
	12 pm
	1 pm
	2 pm
	3 pm
	4 pm
	5 pm
	6 pm
	7 pm
	8 pm
	9 pm

Date:

SCRIPTURE – DRAW CLOSER TO THE KING OF KINGS: Use your name in the place of a character in the scripture you're reading; imagine yourself in that time, using all 5 senses. Pray scripture back to God. Write the scripture down, read it, repeat it out loud throughout the day, memorize it, and meditate on it.

WORSHIP – PRAISE HIM FOR WHO HE IS: How will you glorify and magnify Him today? There is no room here for making personal petitions.

PURE HEART – ASK HIM TO PURIFY YOUR MIND AND HEART: Replace negative thoughts with higher thoughts. God's thoughts are noble, pure, lovely, excellent, right, true, and admirable. Ask God to reveal areas in your life that grieve the Holy Spirit. Confess with a contrite heart and receive forgiveness. As you confess, turn your palms up and release your sin, worry, and anxiety over to God. Now turn your palms down and receive God's love, mercy, favor, and grace.

THANKFULNESS – NAME THOSE THINGS YOU ARE THANKFUL FOR: There's always something to be grateful for. Name them one by one and come back often to rekindle the joy of each one of them.

- O
- O
- O
- O
- O
- O
- O

REFLECTION & REVELATION – PRACTICE LISTENING FOR GOD: God promises that if you draw near to Him, He will tell you things you do not know. Who does God bring to mind? Where is God leading you? Reflect on God's perspective.	TASKS
PRAYER – YOU HAVE NOT BECAUSE YOU ASK NOT: Pray for family, friends, relationships, unity, community, world, church, favor, wisdom, God's will, work, and your future. Pray about anything and everything, without ceasing.	
OBEDIENCE – STAND, SHARE, SERVE: Take steps of faith, and obey promptly. The level of miracles in your life will be directly related to your level of obedience. Faith without works is dead. You have an assignment, a destiny to fulfill.	
	6 am
	7 am
	8 am
	9 am
	10 am
	11 am
	12 pm
	1 pm
	2 pm
	3 pm
	4 pm
	5 pm
	6 pm
	7 pm
	8 pm
	9 pm

Date:

SCRIPTURE – DRAW CLOSER TO THE KING OF KINGS: Use your name in the place of a character in the scripture you're reading; imagine yourself in that time, using all 5 senses. Pray scripture back to God. Write the scripture down, read it, repeat it out loud throughout the day, memorize it, and meditate on it.

WORSHIP – PRAISE HIM FOR WHO HE IS: How will you glorify and magnify Him today? There is no room here for making personal petitions.

PURE HEART – ASK HIM TO PURIFY YOUR MIND AND HEART: Replace negative thoughts with higher thoughts. God's thoughts are noble, pure, lovely, excellent, right, true, and admirable. Ask God to reveal areas in your life that grieve the Holy Spirit. Confess with a contrite heart and receive forgiveness. As you confess, turn your palms up and release your sin, worry, and anxiety over to God. Now turn your palms down and receive God's love, mercy, favor, and grace.

THANKFULNESS – NAME THOSE THINGS YOU ARE THANKFUL FOR: There's always something to be grateful for. Name them one by one and come back often to rekindle the joy of each one of them.

O

O

O

O

O

O

O

REFLECTION & REVELATION – PRACTICE LISTENING FOR GOD: God promises that if you draw near to Him, He will tell you things you do not know. Who does God bring to mind? Where is God leading you? Reflect on God's perspective.	TASKS
PRAYER – YOU HAVE NOT BECAUSE YOU ASK NOT: Pray for family, friends, relationships, unity, community, world, church, favor, wisdom, God's will, work, and your future. Pray about anything and everything, without ceasing.	
OBEDIENCE – STAND, SHARE, SERVE: Take steps of faith, and obey promptly. The level of miracles in your life will be directly related to your level of obedience. Faith without works is dead. You have an assignment, a destiny to fulfill.	
	6 am
	7 am
	8 am
	9 am
	10 am
	11 am
	12 pm
	1 pm
	2 pm
	3 pm
	4 pm
	5 pm
	6 pm
	7 pm
	8 pm
	9 pm

Date:

SCRIPTURE – DRAW CLOSER TO THE KING OF KINGS: Use your name in the place of a character in the scripture you're reading; imagine yourself in that time, using all 5 senses. Pray scripture back to God. Write the scripture down, read it, repeat it out loud throughout the day, memorize it, and meditate on it.

_____
_____
_____
_____
_____
_____
_____
_____
_____
_____
_____
_____

WORSHIP – PRAISE HIM FOR WHO HE IS: How will you glorify and magnify Him today? There is no room here for making personal petitions.

_____
_____
_____
_____

PURE HEART – ASK HIM TO PURIFY YOUR MIND AND HEART: Replace negative thoughts with higher thoughts. God's thoughts are noble, pure, lovely, excellent, right, true, and admirable. Ask God to reveal areas in your life that grieve the Holy Spirit. Confess with a contrite heart and receive forgiveness. As you confess, turn your palms up and release your sin, worry, and anxiety over to God. Now turn your palms down and receive God's love, mercy, favor, and grace.

_____
_____
_____

THANKFULNESS – NAME THOSE THINGS YOU ARE THANKFUL FOR: There's always something to be grateful for. Name them one by one and come back often to rekindle the joy of each one of them.

O
O
O
O
O
O
O

REFLECTION & REVELATION – PRACTICE LISTENING FOR GOD: God promises that if you draw near to Him, He will tell you things you do not know. Who does God bring to mind? Where is God leading you? Reflect on God's perspective.	TASKS
PRAYER – YOU HAVE NOT BECAUSE YOU ASK NOT: Pray for family, friends, relationships, unity, community, world, church, favor, wisdom, God's will, work, and your future. Pray about anything and everything, without ceasing.	
OBEDIENCE – STAND, SHARE, SERVE: Take steps of faith, and obey promptly. The level of miracles in your life will be directly related to your level of obedience. Faith without works is dead. You have an assignment, a destiny to fulfill.	
	6 am
	7 am
	8 am
	9 am
	10 am
	11 am
	12 pm
	1 pm
	2 pm
	3 pm
	4 pm
	5 pm
	6 pm
	7 pm
	8 pm
	9 pm

Date:

SCRIPTURE – DRAW CLOSER TO THE KING OF KINGS: Use your name in the place of a character in the scripture you're reading; imagine yourself in that time, using all 5 senses. Pray scripture back to God. Write the scripture down, read it, repeat it out loud throughout the day, memorize it, and meditate on it.

_____
_____
_____
_____
_____
_____
_____
_____
_____
_____
_____

WORSHIP – PRAISE HIM FOR WHO HE IS: How will you glorify and magnify Him today? There is no room here for making personal petitions.

_____
_____
_____

PURE HEART – ASK HIM TO PURIFY YOUR MIND AND HEART: Replace negative thoughts with higher thoughts. God's thoughts are noble, pure, lovely, excellent, right, true, and admirable. Ask God to reveal areas in your life that grieve the Holy Spirit. Confess with a contrite heart and receive forgiveness. As you confess, turn your palms up and release your sin, worry, and anxiety over to God. Now turn your palms down and receive God's love, mercy, favor, and grace.

_____
_____
_____

THANKFULNESS – NAME THOSE THINGS YOU ARE THANKFUL FOR: There's always something to be grateful for. Name them one by one and come back often to rekindle the joy of each one of them.

O _____

O _____

O _____

O _____

O _____

O _____

O _____

	TASKS
REFLECTION & REVELATION – PRACTICE LISTENING FOR GOD: God promises that if you draw near to Him, He will tell you things you do not know. Who does God bring to mind? Where is God leading you? Reflect on God's perspective.	
PRAYER – YOU HAVE NOT BECAUSE YOU ASK NOT: Pray for family, friends, relationships, unity, community, world, church, favor, wisdom, God's will, work, and your future. Pray about anything and everything, without ceasing.	
OBEDIENCE – STAND, SHARE, SERVE: Take steps of faith, and obey promptly. The level of miracles in your life will be directly related to your level of obedience. Faith without works is dead. You have an assignment, a destiny to fulfill.	
	6 am
	7 am
	8 am
	9 am
	10 am
	11 am
	12 pm
	1 pm
	2 pm
	3 pm
	4 pm
	5 pm
	6 pm
	7 pm
	8 pm
	9 pm

Date:

SCRIPTURE – DRAW CLOSER TO THE KING OF KINGS: Use your name in the place of a character in the scripture you're reading; imagine yourself in that time, using all 5 senses. Pray scripture back to God. Write the scripture down, read it, repeat it out loud throughout the day, memorize it, and meditate on it.

WORSHIP – PRAISE HIM FOR WHO HE IS: How will you glorify and magnify Him today? There is no room here for making personal petitions.

PURE HEART – ASK HIM TO PURIFY YOUR MIND AND HEART: Replace negative thoughts with higher thoughts. God's thoughts are noble, pure, lovely, excellent, right, true, and admirable. Ask God to reveal areas in your life that grieve the Holy Spirit. Confess with a contrite heart and receive forgiveness. As you confess, turn your palms up and release your sin, worry, and anxiety over to God. Now turn your palms down and receive God's love, mercy, favor, and grace.

THANKFULNESS – NAME THOSE THINGS YOU ARE THANKFUL FOR: There's always something to be grateful for. Name them one by one and come back often to rekindle the joy of each one of them.

O

O

O

O

O

O

O

	TASKS
REFLECTION & REVELATION – PRACTICE LISTENING FOR GOD: God promises that if you draw near to Him, He will tell you things you do not know. Who does God bring to mind? Where is God leading you? Reflect on God's perspective.	
PRAYER – YOU HAVE NOT BECAUSE YOU ASK NOT: Pray for family, friends, relationships, unity, community, world, church, favor, wisdom, God's will, work, and your future. Pray about anything and everything, without ceasing.	
OBEDIENCE – STAND, SHARE, SERVE: Take steps of faith, and obey promptly. The level of miracles in your life will be directly related to your level of obedience. Faith without works is dead. You have an assignment, a destiny to fulfill.	
	6 am
	7 am
	8 am
	9 am
	10 am
	11 am
	12 pm
	1 pm
	2 pm
	3 pm
	4 pm
	5 pm
	6 pm
	7 pm
	8 pm
	9 pm

Date:

SCRIPTURE – DRAW CLOSER TO THE KING OF KINGS: Use your name in the place of a character in the scripture you're reading; imagine yourself in that time, using all 5 senses. Pray scripture back to God. Write the scripture down, read it, repeat it out loud throughout the day, memorize it, and meditate on it.

WORSHIP – PRAISE HIM FOR WHO HE IS: How will you glorify and magnify Him today? There is no room here for making personal petitions.

PURE HEART – ASK HIM TO PURIFY YOUR MIND AND HEART: Replace negative thoughts with higher thoughts. God's thoughts are noble, pure, lovely, excellent, right, true, and admirable. Ask God to reveal areas in your life that grieve the Holy Spirit. Confess with a contrite heart and receive forgiveness. As you confess, turn your palms up and release your sin, worry, and anxiety over to God. Now turn your palms down and receive God's love, mercy, favor, and grace.

THANKFULNESS – NAME THOSE THINGS YOU ARE THANKFUL FOR: There's always something to be grateful for. Name them one by one and come back often to rekindle the joy of each one of them.

O

O

O

O

O

O

O

REFLECTION & REVELATION – PRACTICE LISTENING FOR GOD: God promises that if you draw near to Him, He will tell you things you do not know. Who does God bring to mind? Where is God leading you? Reflect on God's perspective.	TASKS
PRAYER – YOU HAVE NOT BECAUSE YOU ASK NOT: Pray for family, friends, relationships, unity, community, world, church, favor, wisdom, God's will, work, and your future. Pray about anything and everything, without ceasing.	
OBEDIENCE – STAND, SHARE, SERVE: Take steps of faith, and obey promptly. The level of miracles in your life will be directly related to your level of obedience. Faith without works is dead. You have an assignment, a destiny to fulfill.	
	6 am
	7 am
	8 am
	9 am
	10 am
	11 am
	12 pm
	1 pm
	2 pm
	3 pm
	4 pm
	5 pm
	6 pm
	7 pm
	8 pm
	9 pm

WEEKLY FOCUS

Last Week's Reflection
Areas to Celebrate:
Areas to Improve:
What did I learn

This Week's Planning
Plan for joyful occasions. Joy is your strength, refreshment, energy, and beauty. What are you looking forward to this week? Find something to laugh about and share it.
Projects/Areas of focus this week:

- [ ]
- [ ]
- [ ]
- [ ]
- [ ]
- [ ]
- [ ]

AREAS TO SIMPLIFY – where to set godly boundaries

	What is important	What is not important	Why	What are Facts/Feelings	Benefits of continuing/not continuing	Pray about possibilities and solutions
Time						
Energy						
Money						
Relationships						
Possessions						

FASTING: Take authority over what controls me; lean on God; keep Christ-focused
What to fast:
Time to fast:
How to fast:
Check motives:

ADDITIONAL REFLECTION

Date:

SCRIPTURE – DRAW CLOSER TO THE KING OF KINGS: Use your name in the place of a character in the scripture you're reading; imagine yourself in that time, using all 5 senses. Pray scripture back to God. Write the scripture down, read it, repeat it out loud throughout the day, memorize it, and meditate on it.

_____
_____
_____
_____
_____
_____
_____
_____
_____
_____
_____
_____
_____
_____

WORSHIP – PRAISE HIM FOR WHO HE IS: How will you glorify and magnify Him today? There is no room here for making personal petitions.

_____
_____
_____
_____

PURE HEART – ASK HIM TO PURIFY YOUR MIND AND HEART: Replace negative thoughts with higher thoughts. God's thoughts are noble, pure, lovely, excellent, right, true, and admirable. Ask God to reveal areas in your life that grieve the Holy Spirit. Confess with a contrite heart and receive forgiveness. As you confess, turn your palms up and release your sin, worry, and anxiety over to God. Now turn your palms down and receive God's love, mercy, favor, and grace.

_____
_____
_____

THANKFULNESS – NAME THOSE THINGS YOU ARE THANKFUL FOR: There's always something to be grateful for. Name them one by one and come back often to rekindle the joy of each one of them.

O
O
O
O
O
O
O

REFLECTION & REVELATION – PRACTICE LISTENING FOR GOD: God promises that if you draw near to Him, He will tell you things you do not know. Who does God bring to mind? Where is God leading you? Reflect on God's perspective.	TASKS
PRAYER – YOU HAVE NOT BECAUSE YOU ASK NOT: Pray for family, friends, relationships, unity, community, world, church, favor, wisdom, God's will, work, and your future. Pray about anything and everything, without ceasing.	
OBEDIENCE – STAND, SHARE, SERVE: Take steps of faith, and obey promptly. The level of miracles in your life will be directly related to your level of obedience. Faith without works is dead. You have an assignment, a destiny to fulfill.	
	6 am
	7 am
	8 am
	9 am
	10 am
	11 am
	12 pm
	1 pm
	2 pm
	3 pm
	4 pm
	5 pm
	6 pm
	7 pm
	8 pm
	9 pm

Date:

SCRIPTURE – DRAW CLOSER TO THE KING OF KINGS: Use your name in the place of a character in the scripture you're reading; imagine yourself in that time, using all 5 senses. Pray scripture back to God. Write the scripture down, read it, repeat it out loud throughout the day, memorize it, and meditate on it.

WORSHIP – PRAISE HIM FOR WHO HE IS: How will you glorify and magnify Him today? There is no room here for making personal petitions.

PURE HEART – ASK HIM TO PURIFY YOUR MIND AND HEART: Replace negative thoughts with higher thoughts. God's thoughts are noble, pure, lovely, excellent, right, true, and admirable. Ask God to reveal areas in your life that grieve the Holy Spirit. Confess with a contrite heart and receive forgiveness. As you confess, turn your palms up and release your sin, worry, and anxiety over to God. Now turn your palms down and receive God's love, mercy, favor, and grace.

THANKFULNESS – NAME THOSE THINGS YOU ARE THANKFUL FOR: There's always something to be grateful for. Name them one by one and come back often to rekindle the joy of each one of them.

O

O

O

O

O

O

O

REFLECTION & REVELATION – PRACTICE LISTENING FOR GOD: God promises that if you draw near to Him, He will tell you things you do not know. Who does God bring to mind? Where is God leading you? Reflect on God's perspective.	TASKS
PRAYER – YOU HAVE NOT BECAUSE YOU ASK NOT: Pray for family, friends, relationships, unity, community, world, church, favor, wisdom, God's will, work, and your future. Pray about anything and everything, without ceasing.	
OBEDIENCE – STAND, SHARE, SERVE: Take steps of faith, and obey promptly. The level of miracles in your life will be directly related to your level of obedience. Faith without works is dead. You have an assignment, a destiny to fulfill.	
	6 am
	7 am
	8 am
	9 am
	10 am
	11 am
	12 pm
	1 pm
	2 pm
	3 pm
	4 pm
	5 pm
	6 pm
	7 pm
	8 pm
	9 pm

Date:

SCRIPTURE – DRAW CLOSER TO THE KING OF KINGS: Use your name in the place of a character in the scripture you're reading; imagine yourself in that time, using all 5 senses. Pray scripture back to God. Write the scripture down, read it, repeat it out loud throughout the day, memorize it, and meditate on it.

WORSHIP – PRAISE HIM FOR WHO HE IS: How will you glorify and magnify Him today? There is no room here for making personal petitions.

PURE HEART – ASK HIM TO PURIFY YOUR MIND AND HEART: Replace negative thoughts with higher thoughts. God's thoughts are noble, pure, lovely, excellent, right, true, and admirable. Ask God to reveal areas in your life that grieve the Holy Spirit. Confess with a contrite heart and receive forgiveness. As you confess, turn your palms up and release your sin, worry, and anxiety over to God. Now turn your palms down and receive God's love, mercy, favor, and grace.

THANKFULNESS – NAME THOSE THINGS YOU ARE THANKFUL FOR: There's always something to be grateful for. Name them one by one and come back often to rekindle the joy of each one of them.

O

O

O

O

O

O

O

REFLECTION & REVELATION – PRACTICE LISTENING FOR GOD: God promises that if you draw near to Him, He will tell you things you do not know. Who does God bring to mind? Where is God leading you? Reflect on God's perspective.	TASKS
PRAYER – YOU HAVE NOT BECAUSE YOU ASK NOT: Pray for family, friends, relationships, unity, community, world, church, favor, wisdom, God's will, work, and your future. Pray about anything and everything, without ceasing.	
OBEDIENCE – STAND, SHARE, SERVE: Take steps of faith, and obey promptly. The level of miracles in your life will be directly related to your level of obedience. Faith without works is dead. You have an assignment, a destiny to fulfill.	
	6 am
	7 am
	8 am
	9 am
	10 am
	11 am
	12 pm
	1 pm
	2 pm
	3 pm
	4 pm
	5 pm
	6 pm
	7 pm
	8 pm
	9 pm

Date:

SCRIPTURE – DRAW CLOSER TO THE KING OF KINGS: Use your name in the place of a character in the scripture you're reading; imagine yourself in that time, using all 5 senses. Pray scripture back to God. Write the scripture down, read it, repeat it out loud throughout the day, memorize it, and meditate on it.

_____
_____
_____
_____
_____
_____
_____
_____
_____
_____
_____
_____
_____

WORSHIP – PRAISE HIM FOR WHO HE IS: How will you glorify and magnify Him today? There is no room here for making personal petitions.

_____
_____
_____
_____

PURE HEART – ASK HIM TO PURIFY YOUR MIND AND HEART: Replace negative thoughts with higher thoughts. God's thoughts are noble, pure, lovely, excellent, right, true, and admirable. Ask God to reveal areas in your life that grieve the Holy Spirit. Confess with a contrite heart and receive forgiveness. As you confess, turn your palms up and release your sin, worry, and anxiety over to God. Now turn your palms down and receive God's love, mercy, favor, and grace.

_____
_____
_____

THANKFULNESS – NAME THOSE THINGS YOU ARE THANKFUL FOR: There's always something to be grateful for. Name them one by one and come back often to rekindle the joy of each one of them.

O
O
O
O
O
O
O

REFLECTION & REVELATION – PRACTICE LISTENING FOR GOD: God promises that if you draw near to Him, He will tell you things you do not know. Who does God bring to mind? Where is God leading you? Reflect on God's perspective.	TASKS
PRAYER – YOU HAVE NOT BECAUSE YOU ASK NOT: Pray for family, friends, relationships, unity, community, world, church, favor, wisdom, God's will, work, and your future. Pray about anything and everything, without ceasing.	
OBEDIENCE – STAND, SHARE, SERVE: Take steps of faith, and obey promptly. The level of miracles in your life will be directly related to your level of obedience. Faith without works is dead. You have an assignment, a destiny to fulfill.	
	6 am
	7 am
	8 am
	9 am
	10 am
	11 am
	12 pm
	1 pm
	2 pm
	3 pm
	4 pm
	5 pm
	6 pm
	7 pm
	8 pm
	9 pm

Date:

SCRIPTURE – DRAW CLOSER TO THE KING OF KINGS: Use your name in the place of a character in the scripture you're reading; imagine yourself in that time, using all 5 senses. Pray scripture back to God. Write the scripture down, read it, repeat it out loud throughout the day, memorize it, and meditate on it.

WORSHIP – PRAISE HIM FOR WHO HE IS: How will you glorify and magnify Him today? There is no room here for making personal petitions.

PURE HEART – ASK HIM TO PURIFY YOUR MIND AND HEART: Replace negative thoughts with higher thoughts. God's thoughts are noble, pure, lovely, excellent, right, true, and admirable. Ask God to reveal areas in your life that grieve the Holy Spirit. Confess with a contrite heart and receive forgiveness. As you confess, turn your palms up and release your sin, worry, and anxiety over to God. Now turn your palms down and receive God's love, mercy, favor, and grace.

THANKFULNESS – NAME THOSE THINGS YOU ARE THANKFUL FOR: There's always something to be grateful for. Name them one by one and come back often to rekindle the joy of each one of them.

O

O

O

O

O

O

O

REFLECTION & REVELATION – PRACTICE LISTENING FOR GOD: God promises that if you draw near to Him, He will tell you things you do not know. Who does God bring to mind? Where is God leading you? Reflect on God's perspective.	TASKS
PRAYER – YOU HAVE NOT BECAUSE YOU ASK NOT: Pray for family, friends, relationships, unity, community, world, church, favor, wisdom, God's will, work, and your future. Pray about anything and everything, without ceasing.	
OBEDIENCE – STAND, SHARE, SERVE: Take steps of faith, and obey promptly. The level of miracles in your life will be directly related to your level of obedience. Faith without works is dead. You have an assignment, a destiny to fulfill.	
	6 am
	7 am
	8 am
	9 am
	10 am
	11 am
	12 pm
	1 pm
	2 pm
	3 pm
	4 pm
	5 pm
	6 pm
	7 pm
	8 pm
	9 pm

Date:

SCRIPTURE – DRAW CLOSER TO THE KING OF KINGS: Use your name in the place of a character in the scripture you're reading; imagine yourself in that time, using all 5 senses. Pray scripture back to God. Write the scripture down, read it, repeat it out loud throughout the day, memorize it, and meditate on it.

_____
_____
_____
_____
_____
_____
_____
_____
_____
_____
_____
_____

WORSHIP – PRAISE HIM FOR WHO HE IS: How will you glorify and magnify Him today? There is no room here for making personal petitions.

_____
_____
_____

PURE HEART – ASK HIM TO PURIFY YOUR MIND AND HEART: Replace negative thoughts with higher thoughts. God's thoughts are noble, pure, lovely, excellent, right, true, and admirable. Ask God to reveal areas in your life that grieve the Holy Spirit. Confess with a contrite heart and receive forgiveness. As you confess, turn your palms up and release your sin, worry, and anxiety over to God. Now turn your palms down and receive God's love, mercy, favor, and grace.

_____
_____
_____

THANKFULNESS – NAME THOSE THINGS YOU ARE THANKFUL FOR: There's always something to be grateful for. Name them one by one and come back often to rekindle the joy of each one of them.

O _____

O _____

O _____

O _____

O _____

O _____

O _____

REFLECTION & REVELATION – PRACTICE LISTENING FOR GOD: God promises that if you draw near to Him, He will tell you things you do not know. Who does God bring to mind? Where is God leading you? Reflect on God's perspective.	TASKS
PRAYER – YOU HAVE NOT BECAUSE YOU ASK NOT: Pray for family, friends, relationships, unity, community, world, church, favor, wisdom, God's will, work, and your future. Pray about anything and everything, without ceasing.	
OBEDIENCE – STAND, SHARE, SERVE: Take steps of faith, and obey promptly. The level of miracles in your life will be directly related to your level of obedience. Faith without works is dead. You have an assignment, a destiny to fulfill.	
	6 am
	7 am
	8 am
	9 am
	10 am
	11 am
	12 pm
	1 pm
	2 pm
	3 pm
	4 pm
	5 pm
	6 pm
	7 pm
	8 pm
	9 pm

Date:

SCRIPTURE – DRAW CLOSER TO THE KING OF KINGS: Use your name in the place of a character in the scripture you're reading; imagine yourself in that time, using all 5 senses. Pray scripture back to God. Write the scripture down, read it, repeat it out loud throughout the day, memorize it, and meditate on it.

WORSHIP – PRAISE HIM FOR WHO HE IS: How will you glorify and magnify Him today? There is no room here for making personal petitions.

PURE HEART – ASK HIM TO PURIFY YOUR MIND AND HEART: Replace negative thoughts with higher thoughts. God's thoughts are noble, pure, lovely, excellent, right, true, and admirable. Ask God to reveal areas in your life that grieve the Holy Spirit. Confess with a contrite heart and receive forgiveness. As you confess, turn your palms up and release your sin, worry, and anxiety over to God. Now turn your palms down and receive God's love, mercy, favor, and grace.

THANKFULNESS – NAME THOSE THINGS YOU ARE THANKFUL FOR: There's always something to be grateful for. Name them one by one and come back often to rekindle the joy of each one of them.

O

O

O

O

O

O

O

REFLECTION & REVELATION – PRACTICE LISTENING FOR GOD: God promises that if you draw near to Him, He will tell you things you do not know. Who does God bring to mind? Where is God leading you? Reflect on God's perspective.	TASKS
PRAYER – YOU HAVE NOT BECAUSE YOU ASK NOT: Pray for family, friends, relationships, unity, community, world, church, favor, wisdom, God's will, work, and your future. Pray about anything and everything, without ceasing.	
OBEDIENCE – STAND, SHARE, SERVE: Take steps of faith, and obey promptly. The level of miracles in your life will be directly related to your level of obedience. Faith without works is dead. You have an assignment, a destiny to fulfill.	
	6 am
	7 am
	8 am
	9 am
	10 am
	11 am
	12 pm
	1 pm
	2 pm
	3 pm
	4 pm
	5 pm
	6 pm
	7 pm
	8 pm
	9 pm

WEEKLY FOCUS

Last Week's Reflection
Areas to Celebrate:
Areas to Improve:
What did I learn

This Week's Planning
Plan for joyful occasions. Joy is your strength, refreshment, energy, and beauty. What are you looking forward to this week? Find something to laugh about and share it.

Projects/Areas of focus this week:

- [ ]
- [ ]
- [ ]
- [ ]
- [ ]
- [ ]
- [ ]

AREAS TO SIMPLIFY – where to set godly boundaries

	What is important	What is not important	Why	What are Facts/Feelings	Benefits of continuing/not continuing	Pray about possibilities and solutions
Time						
Energy						
Money						
Relationships						
Possessions						

FASTING: Take authority over what controls me; lean on God; keep Christ-focused
What to fast:
Time to fast:
How to fast:
Check motives:

Additional Reflection

Date:

SCRIPTURE – DRAW CLOSER TO THE KING OF KINGS: Use your name in the place of a character in the scripture you're reading; imagine yourself in that time, using all 5 senses. Pray scripture back to God. Write the scripture down, read it, repeat it out loud throughout the day, memorize it, and meditate on it.

_____

_____

_____

_____

_____

_____

_____

_____

_____

_____

_____

WORSHIP – PRAISE HIM FOR WHO HE IS: How will you glorify and magnify Him today? There is no room here for making personal petitions.

_____

_____

_____

_____

PURE HEART – ASK HIM TO PURIFY YOUR MIND AND HEART: Replace negative thoughts with higher thoughts. God's thoughts are noble, pure, lovely, excellent, right, true, and admirable. Ask God to reveal areas in your life that grieve the Holy Spirit. Confess with a contrite heart and receive forgiveness. As you confess, turn your palms up and release your sin, worry, and anxiety over to God. Now turn your palms down and receive God's love, mercy, favor, and grace.

_____

_____

_____

THANKFULNESS – NAME THOSE THINGS YOU ARE THANKFUL FOR: There's always something to be grateful for. Name them one by one and come back often to rekindle the joy of each one of them.

O

O

O

O

O

O

O

REFLECTION & REVELATION – PRACTICE LISTENING FOR GOD: God promises that if you draw near to Him, He will tell you things you do not know. Who does God bring to mind? Where is God leading you? Reflect on God's perspective.	TASKS
PRAYER – YOU HAVE NOT BECAUSE YOU ASK NOT: Pray for family, friends, relationships, unity, community, world, church, favor, wisdom, God's will, work, and your future. Pray about anything and everything, without ceasing.	
OBEDIENCE – STAND, SHARE, SERVE: Take steps of faith, and obey promptly. The level of miracles in your life will be directly related to your level of obedience. Faith without works is dead. You have an assignment, a destiny to fulfill.	
	6 am
	7 am
	8 am
	9 am
	10 am
	11 am
	12 pm
	1 pm
	2 pm
	3 pm
	4 pm
	5 pm
	6 pm
	7 pm
	8 pm
	9 pm

Date:

SCRIPTURE – DRAW CLOSER TO THE KING OF KINGS: Use your name in the place of a character in the scripture you're reading; imagine yourself in that time, using all 5 senses. Pray scripture back to God. Write the scripture down, read it, repeat it out loud throughout the day, memorize it, and meditate on it.

_____
_____
_____
_____
_____
_____
_____
_____
_____
_____
_____
_____

WORSHIP – PRAISE HIM FOR WHO HE IS: How will you glorify and magnify Him today? There is no room here for making personal petitions.

_____
_____
_____
_____

PURE HEART – ASK HIM TO PURIFY YOUR MIND AND HEART: Replace negative thoughts with higher thoughts. God's thoughts are noble, pure, lovely, excellent, right, true, and admirable. Ask God to reveal areas in your life that grieve the Holy Spirit. Confess with a contrite heart and receive forgiveness. As you confess, turn your palms up and release your sin, worry, and anxiety over to God. Now turn your palms down and receive God's love, mercy, favor, and grace.

_____
_____
_____

THANKFULNESS – NAME THOSE THINGS YOU ARE THANKFUL FOR: There's always something to be grateful for. Name them one by one and come back often to rekindle the joy of each one of them.

O
O
O
O
O
O
O

REFLECTION & REVELATION – PRACTICE LISTENING FOR GOD: God promises that if you draw near to Him, He will tell you things you do not know. Who does God bring to mind? Where is God leading you? Reflect on God's perspective.	TASKS
PRAYER – YOU HAVE NOT BECAUSE YOU ASK NOT: Pray for family, friends, relationships, unity, community, world, church, favor, wisdom, God's will, work, and your future. Pray about anything and everything, without ceasing.	
OBEDIENCE – STAND, SHARE, SERVE: Take steps of faith, and obey promptly. The level of miracles in your life will be directly related to your level of obedience. Faith without works is dead. You have an assignment, a destiny to fulfill.	
	6 am
	7 am
	8 am
	9 am
	10 am
	11 am
	12 pm
	1 pm
	2 pm
	3 pm
	4 pm
	5 pm
	6 pm
	7 pm
	8 pm
	9 pm

Date:

SCRIPTURE – DRAW CLOSER TO THE KING OF KINGS: Use your name in the place of a character in the scripture you're reading; imagine yourself in that time, using all 5 senses. Pray scripture back to God. Write the scripture down, read it, repeat it out loud throughout the day, memorize it, and meditate on it.

_____
_____
_____
_____
_____
_____
_____
_____
_____
_____
_____
_____

WORSHIP – PRAISE HIM FOR WHO HE IS: How will you glorify and magnify Him today? There is no room here for making personal petitions.

_____
_____
_____
_____

PURE HEART – ASK HIM TO PURIFY YOUR MIND AND HEART: Replace negative thoughts with higher thoughts. God's thoughts are noble, pure, lovely, excellent, right, true, and admirable. Ask God to reveal areas in your life that grieve the Holy Spirit. Confess with a contrite heart and receive forgiveness. As you confess, turn your palms up and release your sin, worry, and anxiety over to God. Now turn your palms down and receive God's love, mercy, favor, and grace.

_____
_____

THANKFULNESS – NAME THOSE THINGS YOU ARE THANKFUL FOR: There's always something to be grateful for. Name them one by one and come back often to rekindle the joy of each one of them.

O _____

O _____

O _____

O _____

O _____

O _____

O _____

REFLECTION & REVELATION – PRACTICE LISTENING FOR GOD: God promises that if you draw near to Him, He will tell you things you do not know. Who does God bring to mind? Where is God leading you? Reflect on God's perspective.	TASKS
PRAYER – YOU HAVE NOT BECAUSE YOU ASK NOT: Pray for family, friends, relationships, unity, community, world, church, favor, wisdom, God's will, work, and your future. Pray about anything and everything, without ceasing.	
OBEDIENCE – STAND, SHARE, SERVE: Take steps of faith, and obey promptly. The level of miracles in your life will be directly related to your level of obedience. Faith without works is dead. You have an assignment, a destiny to fulfill.	
	6 am
	7 am
	8 am
	9 am
	10 am
	11 am
	12 pm
	1 pm
	2 pm
	3 pm
	4 pm
	5 pm
	6 pm
	7 pm
	8 pm
	9 pm

Date:

SCRIPTURE – DRAW CLOSER TO THE KING OF KINGS: Use your name in the place of a character in the scripture you're reading; imagine yourself in that time, using all 5 senses. Pray scripture back to God. Write the scripture down, read it, repeat it out loud throughout the day, memorize it, and meditate on it.

WORSHIP – PRAISE HIM FOR WHO HE IS: How will you glorify and magnify Him today? There is no room here for making personal petitions.

PURE HEART – ASK HIM TO PURIFY YOUR MIND AND HEART: Replace negative thoughts with higher thoughts. God's thoughts are noble, pure, lovely, excellent, right, true, and admirable. Ask God to reveal areas in your life that grieve the Holy Spirit. Confess with a contrite heart and receive forgiveness. As you confess, turn your palms up and release your sin, worry, and anxiety over to God. Now turn your palms down and receive God's love, mercy, favor, and grace.

THANKFULNESS – NAME THOSE THINGS YOU ARE THANKFUL FOR: There's always something to be grateful for. Name them one by one and come back often to rekindle the joy of each one of them.

O

O

O

O

O

O

O

REFLECTION & REVELATION – PRACTICE LISTENING FOR GOD: God promises that if you draw near to Him, He will tell you things you do not know. Who does God bring to mind? Where is God leading you? Reflect on God's perspective.	TASKS
PRAYER – YOU HAVE NOT BECAUSE YOU ASK NOT: Pray for family, friends, relationships, unity, community, world, church, favor, wisdom, God's will, work, and your future. Pray about anything and everything, without ceasing.	
OBEDIENCE – STAND, SHARE, SERVE: Take steps of faith, and obey promptly. The level of miracles in your life will be directly related to your level of obedience. Faith without works is dead. You have an assignment, a destiny to fulfill.	
	6 am
	7 am
	8 am
	9 am
	10 am
	11 am
	12 pm
	1 pm
	2 pm
	3 pm
	4 pm
	5 pm
	6 pm
	7 pm
	8 pm
	9 pm

Date:

SCRIPTURE – DRAW CLOSER TO THE KING OF KINGS: Use your name in the place of a character in the scripture you're reading; imagine yourself in that time, using all 5 senses. Pray scripture back to God. Write the scripture down, read it, repeat it out loud throughout the day, memorize it, and meditate on it.

WORSHIP – PRAISE HIM FOR WHO HE IS: How will you glorify and magnify Him today? There is no room here for making personal petitions.

PURE HEART – ASK HIM TO PURIFY YOUR MIND AND HEART: Replace negative thoughts with higher thoughts. God's thoughts are noble, pure, lovely, excellent, right, true, and admirable. Ask God to reveal areas in your life that grieve the Holy Spirit. Confess with a contrite heart and receive forgiveness. As you confess, turn your palms up and release your sin, worry, and anxiety over to God. Now turn your palms down and receive God's love, mercy, favor, and grace.

THANKFULNESS – NAME THOSE THINGS YOU ARE THANKFUL FOR: There's always something to be grateful for. Name them one by one and come back often to rekindle the joy of each one of them.

O

O

O

O

O

O

O

REFLECTION & REVELATION – PRACTICE LISTENING FOR GOD: God promises that if you draw near to Him, He will tell you things you do not know. Who does God bring to mind? Where is God leading you? Reflect on God's perspective.	TASKS
PRAYER – YOU HAVE NOT BECAUSE YOU ASK NOT: Pray for family, friends, relationships, unity, community, world, church, favor, wisdom, God's will, work, and your future. Pray about anything and everything, without ceasing.	
OBEDIENCE – STAND, SHARE, SERVE: Take steps of faith, and obey promptly. The level of miracles in your life will be directly related to your level of obedience. Faith without works is dead. You have an assignment, a destiny to fulfill.	
	6 am
	7 am
	8 am
	9 am
	10 am
	11 am
	12 pm
	1 pm
	2 pm
	3 pm
	4 pm
	5 pm
	6 pm
	7 pm
	8 pm
	9 pm

Date:

SCRIPTURE – DRAW CLOSER TO THE KING OF KINGS: Use your name in the place of a character in the scripture you're reading; imagine yourself in that time, using all 5 senses. Pray scripture back to God. Write the scripture down, read it, repeat it out loud throughout the day, memorize it, and meditate on it.

_____

_____

_____

_____

_____

_____

_____

_____

_____

_____

_____

WORSHIP – PRAISE HIM FOR WHO HE IS: How will you glorify and magnify Him today? There is no room here for making personal petitions.

_____

_____

_____

PURE HEART – ASK HIM TO PURIFY YOUR MIND AND HEART: Replace negative thoughts with higher thoughts. God's thoughts are noble, pure, lovely, excellent, right, true, and admirable. Ask God to reveal areas in your life that grieve the Holy Spirit. Confess with a contrite heart and receive forgiveness. As you confess, turn your palms up and release your sin, worry, and anxiety over to God. Now turn your palms down and receive God's love, mercy, favor, and grace.

_____

_____

_____

THANKFULNESS – NAME THOSE THINGS YOU ARE THANKFUL FOR: There's always something to be grateful for. Name them one by one and come back often to rekindle the joy of each one of them.

O

O

O

O

O

O

O

REFLECTION & REVELATION – PRACTICE LISTENING FOR GOD: God promises that if you draw near to Him, He will tell you things you do not know. Who does God bring to mind? Where is God leading you? Reflect on God's perspective.	TASKS
PRAYER – YOU HAVE NOT BECAUSE YOU ASK NOT: Pray for family, friends, relationships, unity, community, world, church, favor, wisdom, God's will, work, and your future. Pray about anything and everything, without ceasing.	
OBEDIENCE – STAND, SHARE, SERVE: Take steps of faith, and obey promptly. The level of miracles in your life will be directly related to your level of obedience. Faith without works is dead. You have an assignment, a destiny to fulfill.	
	6 am
	7 am
	8 am
	9 am
	10 am
	11 am
	12 pm
	1 pm
	2 pm
	3 pm
	4 pm
	5 pm
	6 pm
	7 pm
	8 pm
	9 pm

Date:

SCRIPTURE – DRAW CLOSER TO THE KING OF KINGS: Use your name in the place of a character in the scripture you're reading; imagine yourself in that time, using all 5 senses. Pray scripture back to God. Write the scripture down, read it, repeat it out loud throughout the day, memorize it, and meditate on it.

_____

_____

_____

_____

_____

_____

_____

_____

_____

_____

_____

_____

WORSHIP – PRAISE HIM FOR WHO HE IS: How will you glorify and magnify Him today? There is no room here for making personal petitions.

_____

_____

_____

PURE HEART – ASK HIM TO PURIFY YOUR MIND AND HEART: Replace negative thoughts with higher thoughts. God's thoughts are noble, pure, lovely, excellent, right, true, and admirable. Ask God to reveal areas in your life that grieve the Holy Spirit. Confess with a contrite heart and receive forgiveness. As you confess, turn your palms up and release your sin, worry, and anxiety over to God. Now turn your palms down and receive God's love, mercy, favor, and grace.

_____

_____

_____

THANKFULNESS – NAME THOSE THINGS YOU ARE THANKFUL FOR: There's always something to be grateful for. Name them one by one and come back often to rekindle the joy of each one of them.

O

O

O

O

O

O

O

REFLECTION & REVELATION – PRACTICE LISTENING FOR GOD: God promises that if you draw near to Him, He will tell you things you do not know. Who does God bring to mind? Where is God leading you? Reflect on God's perspective.	TASKS
PRAYER – YOU HAVE NOT BECAUSE YOU ASK NOT: Pray for family, friends, relationships, unity, community, world, church, favor, wisdom, God's will, work, and your future. Pray about anything and everything, without ceasing.	
OBEDIENCE – STAND, SHARE, SERVE: Take steps of faith, and obey promptly. The level of miracles in your life will be directly related to your level of obedience. Faith without works is dead. You have an assignment, a destiny to fulfill.	
	6 am
	7 am
	8 am
	9 am
	10 am
	11 am
	12 pm
	1 pm
	2 pm
	3 pm
	4 pm
	5 pm
	6 pm
	7 pm
	8 pm
	9 pm

WEEKLY FOCUS

Last Week's Reflection
Areas to Celebrate:
Areas to Improve:
What did I learn

This Week's Planning
Plan for joyful occasions. Joy is your strength, refreshment, energy, and beauty. What are you looking forward to this week? Find something to laugh about and share it.

Projects/Areas of focus this week:

- [ ]
- [ ]
- [ ]
- [ ]
- [ ]
- [ ]
- [ ]

AREAS TO SIMPLIFY – where to set godly boundaries

	What is important	What is not important	Why	What are Facts/Feelings	Benefits of continuing/not continuing	Pray about possibilities and solutions
Time						
Energy						
Money						
Relationships						
Possessions						

FASTING: Take authority over what controls me; lean on God; keep Christ-focused
What to fast:
Time to fast:
How to fast:
Check motives:

ADDITIONAL REFLECTION

Date:

SCRIPTURE – DRAW CLOSER TO THE KING OF KINGS: Use your name in the place of a character in the scripture you're reading; imagine yourself in that time, using all 5 senses. Pray scripture back to God. Write the scripture down, read it, repeat it out loud throughout the day, memorize it, and meditate on it.

_____
_____
_____
_____
_____
_____
_____
_____
_____
_____
_____
_____

WORSHIP – PRAISE HIM FOR WHO HE IS: How will you glorify and magnify Him today? There is no room here for making personal petitions.

_____
_____
_____
_____

PURE HEART – ASK HIM TO PURIFY YOUR MIND AND HEART: Replace negative thoughts with higher thoughts. God's thoughts are noble, pure, lovely, excellent, right, true, and admirable. Ask God to reveal areas in your life that grieve the Holy Spirit. Confess with a contrite heart and receive forgiveness. As you confess, turn your palms up and release your sin, worry, and anxiety over to God. Now turn your palms down and receive God's love, mercy, favor, and grace.

_____
_____
_____
_____

THANKFULNESS – NAME THOSE THINGS YOU ARE THANKFUL FOR: There's always something to be grateful for. Name them one by one and come back often to rekindle the joy of each one of them.

O
O
O
O
O
O
O

REFLECTION & REVELATION – PRACTICE LISTENING FOR GOD: God promises that if you draw near to Him, He will tell you things you do not know. Who does God bring to mind? Where is God leading you? Reflect on God's perspective.	TASKS
PRAYER – YOU HAVE NOT BECAUSE YOU ASK NOT: Pray for family, friends, relationships, unity, community, world, church, favor, wisdom, God's will, work, and your future. Pray about anything and everything, without ceasing.	
OBEDIENCE – STAND, SHARE, SERVE: Take steps of faith, and obey promptly. The level of miracles in your life will be directly related to your level of obedience. Faith without works is dead. You have an assignment, a destiny to fulfill.	
	6 am
	7 am
	8 am
	9 am
	10 am
	11 am
	12 pm
	1 pm
	2 pm
	3 pm
	4 pm
	5 pm
	6 pm
	7 pm
	8 pm
	9 pm

Date:

SCRIPTURE – DRAW CLOSER TO THE KING OF KINGS: Use your name in the place of a character in the scripture you're reading; imagine yourself in that time, using all 5 senses. Pray scripture back to God. Write the scripture down, read it, repeat it out loud throughout the day, memorize it, and meditate on it.

WORSHIP – PRAISE HIM FOR WHO HE IS: How will you glorify and magnify Him today? There is no room here for making personal petitions.

PURE HEART – ASK HIM TO PURIFY YOUR MIND AND HEART: Replace negative thoughts with higher thoughts. God's thoughts are noble, pure, lovely, excellent, right, true, and admirable. Ask God to reveal areas in your life that grieve the Holy Spirit. Confess with a contrite heart and receive forgiveness. As you confess, turn your palms up and release your sin, worry, and anxiety over to God. Now turn your palms down and receive God's love, mercy, favor, and grace.

THANKFULNESS – NAME THOSE THINGS YOU ARE THANKFUL FOR: There's always something to be grateful for. Name them one by one and come back often to rekindle the joy of each one of them.

O

O

O

O

O

O

O

REFLECTION & REVELATION – PRACTICE LISTENING FOR GOD: God promises that if you draw near to Him, He will tell you things you do not know. Who does God bring to mind? Where is God leading you? Reflect on God's perspective.	TASKS
PRAYER – YOU HAVE NOT BECAUSE YOU ASK NOT: Pray for family, friends, relationships, unity, community, world, church, favor, wisdom, God's will, work, and your future. Pray about anything and everything, without ceasing.	
OBEDIENCE – STAND, SHARE, SERVE: Take steps of faith, and obey promptly. The level of miracles in your life will be directly related to your level of obedience. Faith without works is dead. You have an assignment, a destiny to fulfill.	
	6 am
	7 am
	8 am
	9 am
	10 am
	11 am
	12 pm
	1 pm
	2 pm
	3 pm
	4 pm
	5 pm
	6 pm
	7 pm
	8 pm
	9 pm

Date:

SCRIPTURE – DRAW CLOSER TO THE KING OF KINGS: Use your name in the place of a character in the scripture you're reading; imagine yourself in that time, using all 5 senses. Pray scripture back to God. Write the scripture down, read it, repeat it out loud throughout the day, memorize it, and meditate on it.

WORSHIP – PRAISE HIM FOR WHO HE IS: How will you glorify and magnify Him today? There is no room here for making personal petitions.

PURE HEART – ASK HIM TO PURIFY YOUR MIND AND HEART: Replace negative thoughts with higher thoughts. God's thoughts are noble, pure, lovely, excellent, right, true, and admirable. Ask God to reveal areas in your life that grieve the Holy Spirit. Confess with a contrite heart and receive forgiveness. As you confess, turn your palms up and release your sin, worry, and anxiety over to God. Now turn your palms down and receive God's love, mercy, favor, and grace.

THANKFULNESS – NAME THOSE THINGS YOU ARE THANKFUL FOR: There's always something to be grateful for. Name them one by one and come back often to rekindle the joy of each one of them.

O

O

O

O

O

O

O

REFLECTION & REVELATION – PRACTICE LISTENING FOR GOD: God promises that if you draw near to Him, He will tell you things you do not know. Who does God bring to mind? Where is God leading you? Reflect on God's perspective.	TASKS
PRAYER – YOU HAVE NOT BECAUSE YOU ASK NOT: Pray for family, friends, relationships, unity, community, world, church, favor, wisdom, God's will, work, and your future. Pray about anything and everything, without ceasing.	
OBEDIENCE – STAND, SHARE, SERVE: Take steps of faith, and obey promptly. The level of miracles in your life will be directly related to your level of obedience. Faith without works is dead. You have an assignment, a destiny to fulfill.	
	6 am
	7 am
	8 am
	9 am
	10 am
	11 am
	12 pm
	1 pm
	2 pm
	3 pm
	4 pm
	5 pm
	6 pm
	7 pm
	8 pm
	9 pm

Date:

SCRIPTURE – DRAW CLOSER TO THE KING OF KINGS: Use your name in the place of a character in the scripture you're reading; imagine yourself in that time, using all 5 senses. Pray scripture back to God. Write the scripture down, read it, repeat it out loud throughout the day, memorize it, and meditate on it.

WORSHIP – PRAISE HIM FOR WHO HE IS: How will you glorify and magnify Him today? There is no room here for making personal petitions.

PURE HEART – ASK HIM TO PURIFY YOUR MIND AND HEART: Replace negative thoughts with higher thoughts. God's thoughts are noble, pure, lovely, excellent, right, true, and admirable. Ask God to reveal areas in your life that grieve the Holy Spirit. Confess with a contrite heart and receive forgiveness. As you confess, turn your palms up and release your sin, worry, and anxiety over to God. Now turn your palms down and receive God's love, mercy, favor, and grace.

THANKFULNESS – NAME THOSE THINGS YOU ARE THANKFUL FOR: There's always something to be grateful for. Name them one by one and come back often to rekindle the joy of each one of them.

O

O

O

O

O

O

O

REFLECTION & REVELATION – PRACTICE LISTENING FOR GOD: God promises that if you draw near to Him, He will tell you things you do not know. Who does God bring to mind? Where is God leading you? Reflect on God's perspective.	TASKS
PRAYER – YOU HAVE NOT BECAUSE YOU ASK NOT: Pray for family, friends, relationships, unity, community, world, church, favor, wisdom, God's will, work, and your future. Pray about anything and everything, without ceasing.	
OBEDIENCE – STAND, SHARE, SERVE: Take steps of faith, and obey promptly. The level of miracles in your life will be directly related to your level of obedience. Faith without works is dead. You have an assignment, a destiny to fulfill.	
	6 am
	7 am
	8 am
	9 am
	10 am
	11 am
	12 pm
	1 pm
	2 pm
	3 pm
	4 pm
	5 pm
	6 pm
	7 pm
	8 pm
	9 pm

Date:

SCRIPTURE – DRAW CLOSER TO THE KING OF KINGS: Use your name in the place of a character in the scripture you're reading; imagine yourself in that time, using all 5 senses. Pray scripture back to God. Write the scripture down, read it, repeat it out loud throughout the day, memorize it, and meditate on it.

WORSHIP – PRAISE HIM FOR WHO HE IS: How will you glorify and magnify Him today? There is no room here for making personal petitions.

PURE HEART – ASK HIM TO PURIFY YOUR MIND AND HEART: Replace negative thoughts with higher thoughts. God's thoughts are noble, pure, lovely, excellent, right, true, and admirable. Ask God to reveal areas in your life that grieve the Holy Spirit. Confess with a contrite heart and receive forgiveness. As you confess, turn your palms up and release your sin, worry, and anxiety over to God. Now turn your palms down and receive God's love, mercy, favor, and grace.

THANKFULNESS – NAME THOSE THINGS YOU ARE THANKFUL FOR: There's always something to be grateful for. Name them one by one and come back often to rekindle the joy of each one of them.

O

O

O

O

O

O

O

REFLECTION & REVELATION – PRACTICE LISTENING FOR GOD: God promises that if you draw near to Him, He will tell you things you do not know. Who does God bring to mind? Where is God leading you? Reflect on God's perspective.	TASKS
PRAYER – YOU HAVE NOT BECAUSE YOU ASK NOT: Pray for family, friends, relationships, unity, community, world, church, favor, wisdom, God's will, work, and your future. Pray about anything and everything, without ceasing.	
OBEDIENCE – STAND, SHARE, SERVE: Take steps of faith, and obey promptly. The level of miracles in your life will be directly related to your level of obedience. Faith without works is dead. You have an assignment, a destiny to fulfill.	
	6 am
	7 am
	8 am
	9 am
	10 am
	11 am
	12 pm
	1 pm
	2 pm
	3 pm
	4 pm
	5 pm
	6 pm
	7 pm
	8 pm
	9 pm

Date:

SCRIPTURE – DRAW CLOSER TO THE KING OF KINGS: Use your name in the place of a character in the scripture you're reading; imagine yourself in that time, using all 5 senses. Pray scripture back to God. Write the scripture down, read it, repeat it out loud throughout the day, memorize it, and meditate on it.

WORSHIP – PRAISE HIM FOR WHO HE IS: How will you glorify and magnify Him today? There is no room here for making personal petitions.

PURE HEART – ASK HIM TO PURIFY YOUR MIND AND HEART: Replace negative thoughts with higher thoughts. God's thoughts are noble, pure, lovely, excellent, right, true, and admirable. Ask God to reveal areas in your life that grieve the Holy Spirit. Confess with a contrite heart and receive forgiveness. As you confess, turn your palms up and release your sin, worry, and anxiety over to God. Now turn your palms down and receive God's love, mercy, favor, and grace.

THANKFULNESS – NAME THOSE THINGS YOU ARE THANKFUL FOR: There's always something to be grateful for. Name them one by one and come back often to rekindle the joy of each one of them.

O

O

O

O

O

O

O

REFLECTION & REVELATION – PRACTICE LISTENING FOR GOD: God promises that if you draw near to Him, He will tell you things you do not know. Who does God bring to mind? Where is God leading you? Reflect on God's perspective.	TASKS
PRAYER – YOU HAVE NOT BECAUSE YOU ASK NOT: Pray for family, friends, relationships, unity, community, world, church, favor, wisdom, God's will, work, and your future. Pray about anything and everything, without ceasing.	
OBEDIENCE – STAND, SHARE, SERVE: Take steps of faith, and obey promptly. The level of miracles in your life will be directly related to your level of obedience. Faith without works is dead. You have an assignment, a destiny to fulfill.	
	6 am
	7 am
	8 am
	9 am
	10 am
	11 am
	12 pm
	1 pm
	2 pm
	3 pm
	4 pm
	5 pm
	6 pm
	7 pm
	8 pm
	9 pm

Date:

SCRIPTURE – DRAW CLOSER TO THE KING OF KINGS: Use your name in the place of a character in the scripture you're reading; imagine yourself in that time, using all 5 senses. Pray scripture back to God. Write the scripture down, read it, repeat it out loud throughout the day, memorize it, and meditate on it.

_____
_____
_____
_____
_____
_____
_____
_____
_____
_____
_____
_____

WORSHIP – PRAISE HIM FOR WHO HE IS: How will you glorify and magnify Him today? There is no room here for making personal petitions.

_____
_____
_____
_____

PURE HEART – ASK HIM TO PURIFY YOUR MIND AND HEART: Replace negative thoughts with higher thoughts. God's thoughts are noble, pure, lovely, excellent, right, true, and admirable. Ask God to reveal areas in your life that grieve the Holy Spirit. Confess with a contrite heart and receive forgiveness. As you confess, turn your palms up and release your sin, worry, and anxiety over to God. Now turn your palms down and receive God's love, mercy, favor, and grace.

_____
_____
_____

THANKFULNESS – NAME THOSE THINGS YOU ARE THANKFUL FOR: There's always something to be grateful for. Name them one by one and come back often to rekindle the joy of each one of them.

O

O

O

O

O

O

O

REFLECTION & REVELATION – PRACTICE LISTENING FOR GOD: God promises that if you draw near to Him, He will tell you things you do not know. Who does God bring to mind? Where is God leading you? Reflect on God's perspective.	TASKS
PRAYER – YOU HAVE NOT BECAUSE YOU ASK NOT: Pray for family, friends, relationships, unity, community, world, church, favor, wisdom, God's will, work, and your future. Pray about anything and everything, without ceasing.	
OBEDIENCE – STAND, SHARE, SERVE: Take steps of faith, and obey promptly. The level of miracles in your life will be directly related to your level of obedience. Faith without works is dead. You have an assignment, a destiny to fulfill.	
	6 am
	7 am
	8 am
	9 am
	10 am
	11 am
	12 pm
	1 pm
	2 pm
	3 pm
	4 pm
	5 pm
	6 pm
	7 pm
	8 pm
	9 pm

WEEKLY FOCUS

Last Week's Reflection

Areas to Celebrate:

Areas to Improve:

What did I learn

This Week's Planning

Plan for joyful occasions. Joy is your strength, refreshment, energy, and beauty. What are you looking forward to this week? Find something to laugh about and share it.

Projects/Areas of focus this week:

- ☐
- ☐
- ☐
- ☐
- ☐
- ☐
- ☐

AREAS TO SIMPLIFY – where to set godly boundaries

	What is important	What is not important	Why	What are Facts/Feelings	Benefits of continuing/not continuing	Pray about possibilities and solutions
Time						
Energy						
Money						
Relationships						
Possessions						

FASTING: Take authority over what controls me; lean on God; keep Christ-focused
What to fast:
Time to fast:
How to fast:
Check motives:

ADDITIONAL REFLECTION

Date:

SCRIPTURE – DRAW CLOSER TO THE KING OF KINGS: Use your name in the place of a character in the scripture you're reading; imagine yourself in that time, using all 5 senses. Pray scripture back to God. Write the scripture down, read it, repeat it out loud throughout the day, memorize it, and meditate on it.

WORSHIP – PRAISE HIM FOR WHO HE IS: How will you glorify and magnify Him today? There is no room here for making personal petitions.

PURE HEART – ASK HIM TO PURIFY YOUR MIND AND HEART: Replace negative thoughts with higher thoughts. God's thoughts are noble, pure, lovely, excellent, right, true, and admirable. Ask God to reveal areas in your life that grieve the Holy Spirit. Confess with a contrite heart and receive forgiveness. As you confess, turn your palms up and release your sin, worry, and anxiety over to God. Now turn your palms down and receive God's love, mercy, favor, and grace.

THANKFULNESS – NAME THOSE THINGS YOU ARE THANKFUL FOR: There's always something to be grateful for. Name them one by one and come back often to rekindle the joy of each one of them.

O

O

O

O

O

O

O

REFLECTION & REVELATION – PRACTICE LISTENING FOR GOD: God promises that if you draw near to Him, He will tell you things you do not know. Who does God bring to mind? Where is God leading you? Reflect on God's perspective.	TASKS
PRAYER – YOU HAVE NOT BECAUSE YOU ASK NOT: Pray for family, friends, relationships, unity, community, world, church, favor, wisdom, God's will, work, and your future. Pray about anything and everything, without ceasing.	
OBEDIENCE – STAND, SHARE, SERVE: Take steps of faith, and obey promptly. The level of miracles in your life will be directly related to your level of obedience. Faith without works is dead. You have an assignment, a destiny to fulfill.	
	6 am
	7 am
	8 am
	9 am
	10 am
	11 am
	12 pm
	1 pm
	2 pm
	3 pm
	4 pm
	5 pm
	6 pm
	7 pm
	8 pm
	9 pm

Date:

SCRIPTURE – DRAW CLOSER TO THE KING OF KINGS: Use your name in the place of a character in the scripture you're reading; imagine yourself in that time, using all 5 senses. Pray scripture back to God. Write the scripture down, read it, repeat it out loud throughout the day, memorize it, and meditate on it.

WORSHIP – PRAISE HIM FOR WHO HE IS: How will you glorify and magnify Him today? There is no room here for making personal petitions.

PURE HEART – ASK HIM TO PURIFY YOUR MIND AND HEART: Replace negative thoughts with higher thoughts. God's thoughts are noble, pure, lovely, excellent, right, true, and admirable. Ask God to reveal areas in your life that grieve the Holy Spirit. Confess with a contrite heart and receive forgiveness. As you confess, turn your palms up and release your sin, worry, and anxiety over to God. Now turn your palms down and receive God's love, mercy, favor, and grace.

THANKFULNESS – NAME THOSE THINGS YOU ARE THANKFUL FOR: There's always something to be grateful for. Name them one by one and come back often to rekindle the joy of each one of them.

O

O

O

O

O

O

O

REFLECTION & REVELATION – PRACTICE LISTENING FOR GOD: God promises that if you draw near to Him, He will tell you things you do not know. Who does God bring to mind? Where is God leading you? Reflect on God's perspective.	TASKS
PRAYER – YOU HAVE NOT BECAUSE YOU ASK NOT: Pray for family, friends, relationships, unity, community, world, church, favor, wisdom, God's will, work, and your future. Pray about anything and everything, without ceasing.	
OBEDIENCE – STAND, SHARE, SERVE: Take steps of faith, and obey promptly. The level of miracles in your life will be directly related to your level of obedience. Faith without works is dead. You have an assignment, a destiny to fulfill.	
	6 am
	7 am
	8 am
	9 am
	10 am
	11 am
	12 pm
	1 pm
	2 pm
	3 pm
	4 pm
	5 pm
	6 pm
	7 pm
	8 pm
	9 pm

Date:

SCRIPTURE – DRAW CLOSER TO THE KING OF KINGS: Use your name in the place of a character in the scripture you're reading; imagine yourself in that time, using all 5 senses. Pray scripture back to God. Write the scripture down, read it, repeat it out loud throughout the day, memorize it, and meditate on it.

_____
_____
_____
_____
_____
_____
_____
_____
_____
_____
_____
_____

WORSHIP – PRAISE HIM FOR WHO HE IS: How will you glorify and magnify Him today? There is no room here for making personal petitions.

_____
_____
_____
_____

PURE HEART – ASK HIM TO PURIFY YOUR MIND AND HEART: Replace negative thoughts with higher thoughts. God's thoughts are noble, pure, lovely, excellent, right, true, and admirable. Ask God to reveal areas in your life that grieve the Holy Spirit. Confess with a contrite heart and receive forgiveness. As you confess, turn your palms up and release your sin, worry, and anxiety over to God. Now turn your palms down and receive God's love, mercy, favor, and grace.

_____
_____
_____
_____

THANKFULNESS – NAME THOSE THINGS YOU ARE THANKFUL FOR: There's always something to be grateful for. Name them one by one and come back often to rekindle the joy of each one of them.

O
O
O
O
O
O
O

REFLECTION & REVELATION – PRACTICE LISTENING FOR GOD: God promises that if you draw near to Him, He will tell you things you do not know. Who does God bring to mind? Where is God leading you? Reflect on God's perspective.	TASKS
PRAYER – YOU HAVE NOT BECAUSE YOU ASK NOT: Pray for family, friends, relationships, unity, community, world, church, favor, wisdom, God's will, work, and your future. Pray about anything and everything, without ceasing.	
OBEDIENCE – STAND, SHARE, SERVE: Take steps of faith, and obey promptly. The level of miracles in your life will be directly related to your level of obedience. Faith without works is dead. You have an assignment, a destiny to fulfill.	
	6 am
	7 am
	8 am
	9 am
	10 am
	11 am
	12 pm
	1 pm
	2 pm
	3 pm
	4 pm
	5 pm
	6 pm
	7 pm
	8 pm
	9 pm

Date:

SCRIPTURE – DRAW CLOSER TO THE KING OF KINGS: Use your name in the place of a character in the scripture you're reading; imagine yourself in that time, using all 5 senses. Pray scripture back to God. Write the scripture down, read it, repeat it out loud throughout the day, memorize it, and meditate on it.

WORSHIP – PRAISE HIM FOR WHO HE IS: How will you glorify and magnify Him today? There is no room here for making personal petitions.

PURE HEART – ASK HIM TO PURIFY YOUR MIND AND HEART: Replace negative thoughts with higher thoughts. God's thoughts are noble, pure, lovely, excellent, right, true, and admirable. Ask God to reveal areas in your life that grieve the Holy Spirit. Confess with a contrite heart and receive forgiveness. As you confess, turn your palms up and release your sin, worry, and anxiety over to God. Now turn your palms down and receive God's love, mercy, favor, and grace.

THANKFULNESS – NAME THOSE THINGS YOU ARE THANKFUL FOR: There's always something to be grateful for. Name them one by one and come back often to rekindle the joy of each one of them.

O

O

O

O

O

O

O

REFLECTION & REVELATION – PRACTICE LISTENING FOR GOD: God promises that if you draw near to Him, He will tell you things you do not know. Who does God bring to mind? Where is God leading you? Reflect on God's perspective.	TASKS
PRAYER – YOU HAVE NOT BECAUSE YOU ASK NOT: Pray for family, friends, relationships, unity, community, world, church, favor, wisdom, God's will, work, and your future. Pray about anything and everything, without ceasing.	
OBEDIENCE – STAND, SHARE, SERVE: Take steps of faith, and obey promptly. The level of miracles in your life will be directly related to your level of obedience. Faith without works is dead. You have an assignment, a destiny to fulfill.	
	6 am
	7 am
	8 am
	9 am
	10 am
	11 am
	12 pm
	1 pm
	2 pm
	3 pm
	4 pm
	5 pm
	6 pm
	7 pm
	8 pm
	9 pm

Date:

SCRIPTURE – DRAW CLOSER TO THE KING OF KINGS: Use your name in the place of a character in the scripture you're reading; imagine yourself in that time, using all 5 senses. Pray scripture back to God. Write the scripture down, read it, repeat it out loud throughout the day, memorize it, and meditate on it.

_____
_____
_____
_____
_____
_____
_____
_____
_____
_____
_____
_____
_____
_____

WORSHIP – PRAISE HIM FOR WHO HE IS: How will you glorify and magnify Him today? There is no room here for making personal petitions.

_____
_____
_____
_____

PURE HEART – ASK HIM TO PURIFY YOUR MIND AND HEART: Replace negative thoughts with higher thoughts. God's thoughts are noble, pure, lovely, excellent, right, true, and admirable. Ask God to reveal areas in your life that grieve the Holy Spirit. Confess with a contrite heart and receive forgiveness. As you confess, turn your palms up and release your sin, worry, and anxiety over to God. Now turn your palms down and receive God's love, mercy, favor, and grace.

_____
_____
_____

THANKFULNESS – NAME THOSE THINGS YOU ARE THANKFUL FOR: There's always something to be grateful for. Name them one by one and come back often to rekindle the joy of each one of them.

O
O
O
O
O
O
O

REFLECTION & REVELATION – PRACTICE LISTENING FOR GOD: God promises that if you draw near to Him, He will tell you things you do not know. Who does God bring to mind? Where is God leading you? Reflect on God's perspective.	TASKS
PRAYER – YOU HAVE NOT BECAUSE YOU ASK NOT: Pray for family, friends, relationships, unity, community, world, church, favor, wisdom, God's will, work, and your future. Pray about anything and everything, without ceasing.	
OBEDIENCE – STAND, SHARE, SERVE: Take steps of faith, and obey promptly. The level of miracles in your life will be directly related to your level of obedience. Faith without works is dead. You have an assignment, a destiny to fulfill.	
	6 am
	7 am
	8 am
	9 am
	10 am
	11 am
	12 pm
	1 pm
	2 pm
	3 pm
	4 pm
	5 pm
	6 pm
	7 pm
	8 pm
	9 pm

Date:

SCRIPTURE – DRAW CLOSER TO THE KING OF KINGS: Use your name in the place of a character in the scripture you're reading; imagine yourself in that time, using all 5 senses. Pray scripture back to God. Write the scripture down, read it, repeat it out loud throughout the day, memorize it, and meditate on it.

_____
_____
_____
_____
_____
_____
_____
_____
_____
_____
_____
_____
_____
_____

WORSHIP – PRAISE HIM FOR WHO HE IS: How will you glorify and magnify Him today? There is no room here for making personal petitions.

_____
_____
_____

PURE HEART – ASK HIM TO PURIFY YOUR MIND AND HEART: Replace negative thoughts with higher thoughts. God's thoughts are noble, pure, lovely, excellent, right, true, and admirable. Ask God to reveal areas in your life that grieve the Holy Spirit. Confess with a contrite heart and receive forgiveness. As you confess, turn your palms up and release your sin, worry, and anxiety over to God. Now turn your palms down and receive God's love, mercy, favor, and grace.

_____
_____
_____

THANKFULNESS – NAME THOSE THINGS YOU ARE THANKFUL FOR: There's always something to be grateful for. Name them one by one and come back often to rekindle the joy of each one of them.

O
O
O
O
O
O
O

REFLECTION & REVELATION – PRACTICE LISTENING FOR GOD: God promises that if you draw near to Him, He will tell you things you do not know. Who does God bring to mind? Where is God leading you? Reflect on God's perspective.	TASKS
PRAYER – YOU HAVE NOT BECAUSE YOU ASK NOT: Pray for family, friends, relationships, unity, community, world, church, favor, wisdom, God's will, work, and your future. Pray about anything and everything, without ceasing.	
OBEDIENCE – STAND, SHARE, SERVE: Take steps of faith, and obey promptly. The level of miracles in your life will be directly related to your level of obedience. Faith without works is dead. You have an assignment, a destiny to fulfill.	
	6 am
	7 am
	8 am
	9 am
	10 am
	11 am
	12 pm
	1 pm
	2 pm
	3 pm
	4 pm
	5 pm
	6 pm
	7 pm
	8 pm
	9 pm

Date:

SCRIPTURE – DRAW CLOSER TO THE KING OF KINGS: Use your name in the place of a character in the scripture you're reading; imagine yourself in that time, using all 5 senses. Pray scripture back to God. Write the scripture down, read it, repeat it out loud throughout the day, memorize it, and meditate on it.

WORSHIP – PRAISE HIM FOR WHO HE IS: How will you glorify and magnify Him today? There is no room here for making personal petitions.

PURE HEART – ASK HIM TO PURIFY YOUR MIND AND HEART: Replace negative thoughts with higher thoughts. God's thoughts are noble, pure, lovely, excellent, right, true, and admirable. Ask God to reveal areas in your life that grieve the Holy Spirit. Confess with a contrite heart and receive forgiveness. As you confess, turn your palms up and release your sin, worry, and anxiety over to God. Now turn your palms down and receive God's love, mercy, favor, and grace.

THANKFULNESS – NAME THOSE THINGS YOU ARE THANKFUL FOR: There's always something to be grateful for. Name them one by one and come back often to rekindle the joy of each one of them.

O

O

O

O

O

O

O

REFLECTION & REVELATION – PRACTICE LISTENING FOR GOD: God promises that if you draw near to Him, He will tell you things you do not know. Who does God bring to mind? Where is God leading you? Reflect on God's perspective.	TASKS
PRAYER – YOU HAVE NOT BECAUSE YOU ASK NOT: Pray for family, friends, relationships, unity, community, world, church, favor, wisdom, God's will, work, and your future. Pray about anything and everything, without ceasing.	
OBEDIENCE – STAND, SHARE, SERVE: Take steps of faith, and obey promptly. The level of miracles in your life will be directly related to your level of obedience. Faith without works is dead. You have an assignment, a destiny to fulfill.	
	6 am
	7 am
	8 am
	9 am
	10 am
	11 am
	12 pm
	1 pm
	2 pm
	3 pm
	4 pm
	5 pm
	6 pm
	7 pm
	8 pm
	9 pm

WEEKLY FOCUS

Last Week's Reflection
Areas to Celebrate:
Areas to Improve:
What did I learn

This Week's Planning
Plan for joyful occasions. Joy is your strength, refreshment, energy, and beauty. What are you looking forward to this week? Find something to laugh about and share it.
Projects/Areas of focus this week:
☐
☐
☐
☐
☐
☐
☐

AREAS TO SIMPLIFY – where to set godly boundaries

	What is important	What is not important	Why	What are Facts/Feelings	Benefits of continuing/not continuing	Pray about possibilities and solutions
Time						
Energy						
Money						
Relationships						
Possessions						

FASTING: Take authority over what controls me; lean on God; keep Christ-focused
What to fast:
Time to fast:
How to fast:
Check motives:

ADDITIONAL REFLECTION

Date:

SCRIPTURE – DRAW CLOSER TO THE KING OF KINGS: Use your name in the place of a character in the scripture you're reading; imagine yourself in that time, using all 5 senses. Pray scripture back to God. Write the scripture down, read it, repeat it out loud throughout the day, memorize it, and meditate on it.

WORSHIP – PRAISE HIM FOR WHO HE IS: How will you glorify and magnify Him today? There is no room here for making personal petitions.

PURE HEART – ASK HIM TO PURIFY YOUR MIND AND HEART: Replace negative thoughts with higher thoughts. God's thoughts are noble, pure, lovely, excellent, right, true, and admirable. Ask God to reveal areas in your life that grieve the Holy Spirit. Confess with a contrite heart and receive forgiveness. As you confess, turn your palms up and release your sin, worry, and anxiety over to God. Now turn your palms down and receive God's love, mercy, favor, and grace.

THANKFULNESS – NAME THOSE THINGS YOU ARE THANKFUL FOR: There's always something to be grateful for. Name them one by one and come back often to rekindle the joy of each one of them.

O

O

O

O

O

O

O

REFLECTION & REVELATION – PRACTICE LISTENING FOR GOD: God promises that if you draw near to Him, He will tell you things you do not know. Who does God bring to mind? Where is God leading you? Reflect on God's perspective.	TASKS
PRAYER – YOU HAVE NOT BECAUSE YOU ASK NOT: Pray for family, friends, relationships, unity, community, world, church, favor, wisdom, God's will, work, and your future. Pray about anything and everything, without ceasing.	
OBEDIENCE – STAND, SHARE, SERVE: Take steps of faith, and obey promptly. The level of miracles in your life will be directly related to your level of obedience. Faith without works is dead. You have an assignment, a destiny to fulfill.	
	6 am
	7 am
	8 am
	9 am
	10 am
	11 am
	12 pm
	1 pm
	2 pm
	3 pm
	4 pm
	5 pm
	6 pm
	7 pm
	8 pm
	9 pm

Date:

SCRIPTURE – DRAW CLOSER TO THE KING OF KINGS: Use your name in the place of a character in the scripture you're reading; imagine yourself in that time, using all 5 senses. Pray scripture back to God. Write the scripture down, read it, repeat it out loud throughout the day, memorize it, and meditate on it.

_____
_____
_____
_____
_____
_____
_____
_____
_____
_____
_____
_____
_____

WORSHIP – PRAISE HIM FOR WHO HE IS: How will you glorify and magnify Him today? There is no room here for making personal petitions.

_____
_____
_____

PURE HEART – ASK HIM TO PURIFY YOUR MIND AND HEART: Replace negative thoughts with higher thoughts. God's thoughts are noble, pure, lovely, excellent, right, true, and admirable. Ask God to reveal areas in your life that grieve the Holy Spirit. Confess with a contrite heart and receive forgiveness. As you confess, turn your palms up and release your sin, worry, and anxiety over to God. Now turn your palms down and receive God's love, mercy, favor, and grace.

_____
_____
_____

THANKFULNESS – NAME THOSE THINGS YOU ARE THANKFUL FOR: There's always something to be grateful for. Name them one by one and come back often to rekindle the joy of each one of them.

O
O
O
O
O
O
O

	TASKS
REFLECTION & REVELATION – PRACTICE LISTENING FOR GOD: God promises that if you draw near to Him, He will tell you things you do not know. Who does God bring to mind? Where is God leading you? Reflect on God's perspective.	
PRAYER – YOU HAVE NOT BECAUSE YOU ASK NOT: Pray for family, friends, relationships, unity, community, world, church, favor, wisdom, God's will, work, and your future. Pray about anything and everything, without ceasing.	
OBEDIENCE – STAND, SHARE, SERVE: Take steps of faith, and obey promptly. The level of miracles in your life will be directly related to your level of obedience. Faith without works is dead. You have an assignment, a destiny to fulfill.	
	6 am
	7 am
	8 am
	9 am
	10 am
	11 am
	12 pm
	1 pm
	2 pm
	3 pm
	4 pm
	5 pm
	6 pm
	7 pm
	8 pm
	9 pm

Date:

SCRIPTURE – DRAW CLOSER TO THE KING OF KINGS: Use your name in the place of a character in the scripture you're reading; imagine yourself in that time, using all 5 senses. Pray scripture back to God. Write the scripture down, read it, repeat it out loud throughout the day, memorize it, and meditate on it.

_____

_____

_____

_____

_____

_____

_____

_____

_____

_____

_____

_____

WORSHIP – PRAISE HIM FOR WHO HE IS: How will you glorify and magnify Him today? There is no room here for making personal petitions.

_____

_____

_____

PURE HEART – ASK HIM TO PURIFY YOUR MIND AND HEART: Replace negative thoughts with higher thoughts. God's thoughts are noble, pure, lovely, excellent, right, true, and admirable. Ask God to reveal areas in your life that grieve the Holy Spirit. Confess with a contrite heart and receive forgiveness. As you confess, turn your palms up and release your sin, worry, and anxiety over to God. Now turn your palms down and receive God's love, mercy, favor, and grace.

_____

_____

_____

THANKFULNESS – NAME THOSE THINGS YOU ARE THANKFUL FOR: There's always something to be grateful for. Name them one by one and come back often to rekindle the joy of each one of them.

O

O

O

O

O

O

O

REFLECTION & REVELATION – PRACTICE LISTENING FOR GOD: God promises that if you draw near to Him, He will tell you things you do not know. Who does God bring to mind? Where is God leading you? Reflect on God's perspective.	TASKS
PRAYER – YOU HAVE NOT BECAUSE YOU ASK NOT: Pray for family, friends, relationships, unity, community, world, church, favor, wisdom, God's will, work, and your future. Pray about anything and everything, without ceasing.	
OBEDIENCE – STAND, SHARE, SERVE: Take steps of faith, and obey promptly. The level of miracles in your life will be directly related to your level of obedience. Faith without works is dead. You have an assignment, a destiny to fulfill.	
	6 am
	7 am
	8 am
	9 am
	10 am
	11 am
	12 pm
	1 pm
	2 pm
	3 pm
	4 pm
	5 pm
	6 pm
	7 pm
	8 pm
	9 pm

Date:

SCRIPTURE – DRAW CLOSER TO THE KING OF KINGS: Use your name in the place of a character in the scripture you're reading; imagine yourself in that time, using all 5 senses. Pray scripture back to God. Write the scripture down, read it, repeat it out loud throughout the day, memorize it, and meditate on it.

WORSHIP – PRAISE HIM FOR WHO HE IS: How will you glorify and magnify Him today? There is no room here for making personal petitions.

PURE HEART – ASK HIM TO PURIFY YOUR MIND AND HEART: Replace negative thoughts with higher thoughts. God's thoughts are noble, pure, lovely, excellent, right, true, and admirable. Ask God to reveal areas in your life that grieve the Holy Spirit. Confess with a contrite heart and receive forgiveness. As you confess, turn your palms up and release your sin, worry, and anxiety over to God. Now turn your palms down and receive God's love, mercy, favor, and grace.

THANKFULNESS – NAME THOSE THINGS YOU ARE THANKFUL FOR: There's always something to be grateful for. Name them one by one and come back often to rekindle the joy of each one of them.

O

O

O

O

O

O

O

REFLECTION & REVELATION – PRACTICE LISTENING FOR GOD: God promises that if you draw near to Him, He will tell you things you do not know. Who does God bring to mind? Where is God leading you? Reflect on God's perspective.	TASKS
PRAYER – YOU HAVE NOT BECAUSE YOU ASK NOT: Pray for family, friends, relationships, unity, community, world, church, favor, wisdom, God's will, work, and your future. Pray about anything and everything, without ceasing.	
OBEDIENCE – STAND, SHARE, SERVE: Take steps of faith, and obey promptly. The level of miracles in your life will be directly related to your level of obedience. Faith without works is dead. You have an assignment, a destiny to fulfill.	
	6 am
	7 am
	8 am
	9 am
	10 am
	11 am
	12 pm
	1 pm
	2 pm
	3 pm
	4 pm
	5 pm
	6 pm
	7 pm
	8 pm
	9 pm

Date:

SCRIPTURE – DRAW CLOSER TO THE KING OF KINGS: Use your name in the place of a character in the scripture you're reading; imagine yourself in that time, using all 5 senses. Pray scripture back to God. Write the scripture down, read it, repeat it out loud throughout the day, memorize it, and meditate on it.

_____
_____
_____
_____
_____
_____
_____
_____
_____
_____
_____
_____
_____

WORSHIP – PRAISE HIM FOR WHO HE IS: How will you glorify and magnify Him today? There is no room here for making personal petitions.

_____
_____
_____
_____

PURE HEART – ASK HIM TO PURIFY YOUR MIND AND HEART: Replace negative thoughts with higher thoughts. God's thoughts are noble, pure, lovely, excellent, right, true, and admirable. Ask God to reveal areas in your life that grieve the Holy Spirit. Confess with a contrite heart and receive forgiveness. As you confess, turn your palms up and release your sin, worry, and anxiety over to God. Now turn your palms down and receive God's love, mercy, favor, and grace.

_____
_____
_____

THANKFULNESS – NAME THOSE THINGS YOU ARE THANKFUL FOR: There's always something to be grateful for. Name them one by one and come back often to rekindle the joy of each one of them.

O _____

O _____

O _____

O _____

O _____

O _____

O _____

REFLECTION & REVELATION – PRACTICE LISTENING FOR GOD: God promises that if you draw near to Him, He will tell you things you do not know. Who does God bring to mind? Where is God leading you? Reflect on God's perspective.	TASKS
PRAYER – YOU HAVE NOT BECAUSE YOU ASK NOT: Pray for family, friends, relationships, unity, community, world, church, favor, wisdom, God's will, work, and your future. Pray about anything and everything, without ceasing.	
OBEDIENCE – STAND, SHARE, SERVE: Take steps of faith, and obey promptly. The level of miracles in your life will be directly related to your level of obedience. Faith without works is dead. You have an assignment, a destiny to fulfill.	
	6 am
	7 am
	8 am
	9 am
	10 am
	11 am
	12 pm
	1 pm
	2 pm
	3 pm
	4 pm
	5 pm
	6 pm
	7 pm
	8 pm
	9 pm

Date:

SCRIPTURE – DRAW CLOSER TO THE KING OF KINGS: Use your name in the place of a character in the scripture you're reading; imagine yourself in that time, using all 5 senses. Pray scripture back to God. Write the scripture down, read it, repeat it out loud throughout the day, memorize it, and meditate on it.

WORSHIP – PRAISE HIM FOR WHO HE IS: How will you glorify and magnify Him today? There is no room here for making personal petitions.

PURE HEART – ASK HIM TO PURIFY YOUR MIND AND HEART: Replace negative thoughts with higher thoughts. God's thoughts are noble, pure, lovely, excellent, right, true, and admirable. Ask God to reveal areas in your life that grieve the Holy Spirit. Confess with a contrite heart and receive forgiveness. As you confess, turn your palms up and release your sin, worry, and anxiety over to God. Now turn your palms down and receive God's love, mercy, favor, and grace.

THANKFULNESS – NAME THOSE THINGS YOU ARE THANKFUL FOR: There's always something to be grateful for. Name them one by one and come back often to rekindle the joy of each one of them.

O

O

O

O

O

O

O

REFLECTION & REVELATION – PRACTICE LISTENING FOR GOD: God promises that if you draw near to Him, He will tell you things you do not know. Who does God bring to mind? Where is God leading you? Reflect on God's perspective.	TASKS
PRAYER – YOU HAVE NOT BECAUSE YOU ASK NOT: Pray for family, friends, relationships, unity, community, world, church, favor, wisdom, God's will, work, and your future. Pray about anything and everything, without ceasing.	
OBEDIENCE – STAND, SHARE, SERVE: Take steps of faith, and obey promptly. The level of miracles in your life will be directly related to your level of obedience. Faith without works is dead. You have an assignment, a destiny to fulfill.	
	6 am
	7 am
	8 am
	9 am
	10 am
	11 am
	12 pm
	1 pm
	2 pm
	3 pm
	4 pm
	5 pm
	6 pm
	7 pm
	8 pm
	9 pm

Date:

SCRIPTURE – DRAW CLOSER TO THE KING OF KINGS: Use your name in the place of a character in the scripture you're reading; imagine yourself in that time, using all 5 senses. Pray scripture back to God. Write the scripture down, read it, repeat it out loud throughout the day, memorize it, and meditate on it.

WORSHIP – PRAISE HIM FOR WHO HE IS: How will you glorify and magnify Him today? There is no room here for making personal petitions.

PURE HEART – ASK HIM TO PURIFY YOUR MIND AND HEART: Replace negative thoughts with higher thoughts. God's thoughts are noble, pure, lovely, excellent, right, true, and admirable. Ask God to reveal areas in your life that grieve the Holy Spirit. Confess with a contrite heart and receive forgiveness. As you confess, turn your palms up and release your sin, worry, and anxiety over to God. Now turn your palms down and receive God's love, mercy, favor, and grace.

THANKFULNESS – NAME THOSE THINGS YOU ARE THANKFUL FOR: There's always something to be grateful for. Name them one by one and come back often to rekindle the joy of each one of them.

O

O

O

O

O

O

O

	TASKS
REFLECTION & REVELATION – PRACTICE LISTENING FOR GOD: God promises that if you draw near to Him, He will tell you things you do not know. Who does God bring to mind? Where is God leading you? Reflect on God's perspective.	
PRAYER – YOU HAVE NOT BECAUSE YOU ASK NOT: Pray for family, friends, relationships, unity, community, world, church, favor, wisdom, God's will, work, and your future. Pray about anything and everything, without ceasing.	
OBEDIENCE – STAND, SHARE, SERVE: Take steps of faith, and obey promptly. The level of miracles in your life will be directly related to your level of obedience. Faith without works is dead. You have an assignment, a destiny to fulfill.	
	6 am
	7 am
	8 am
	9 am
	10 am
	11 am
	12 pm
	1 pm
	2 pm
	3 pm
	4 pm
	5 pm
	6 pm
	7 pm
	8 pm
	9 pm

WEEKLY FOCUS

Last Week's Reflection
Areas to Celebrate:
Areas to Improve:
What did I learn

This Week's Planning

Plan for joyful occasions. Joy is your strength, refreshment, energy, and beauty. What are you looking forward to this week? Find something to laugh about and share it.

Projects/Areas of focus this week:

☐
☐
☐
☐
☐
☐
☐

AREAS TO SIMPLIFY – where to set godly boundaries

	What is important	What is not important	Why	What are Facts/Feelings	Benefits of continuing/not continuing	Pray about possibilities and solutions
Time						
Energy						
Money						
Relationships						
Possessions						

FASTING: Take authority over what controls me; lean on God; keep Christ-focused
What to fast:
Time to fast:
How to fast:
Check motives:

ADDITIONAL REFLECTION

Date:

SCRIPTURE – DRAW CLOSER TO THE KING OF KINGS: Use your name in the place of a character in the scripture you're reading; imagine yourself in that time, using all 5 senses. Pray scripture back to God. Write the scripture down, read it, repeat it out loud throughout the day, memorize it, and meditate on it.

WORSHIP – PRAISE HIM FOR WHO HE IS: How will you glorify and magnify Him today? There is no room here for making personal petitions.

PURE HEART – ASK HIM TO PURIFY YOUR MIND AND HEART: Replace negative thoughts with higher thoughts. God's thoughts are noble, pure, lovely, excellent, right, true, and admirable. Ask God to reveal areas in your life that grieve the Holy Spirit. Confess with a contrite heart and receive forgiveness. As you confess, turn your palms up and release your sin, worry, and anxiety over to God. Now turn your palms down and receive God's love, mercy, favor, and grace.

THANKFULNESS – NAME THOSE THINGS YOU ARE THANKFUL FOR: There's always something to be grateful for. Name them one by one and come back often to rekindle the joy of each one of them.

O

O

O

O

O

O

O

REFLECTION & REVELATION – PRACTICE LISTENING FOR GOD: God promises that if you draw near to Him, He will tell you things you do not know. Who does God bring to mind? Where is God leading you? Reflect on God's perspective.	TASKS
PRAYER – YOU HAVE NOT BECAUSE YOU ASK NOT: Pray for family, friends, relationships, unity, community, world, church, favor, wisdom, God's will, work, and your future. Pray about anything and everything, without ceasing.	
OBEDIENCE – STAND, SHARE, SERVE: Take steps of faith, and obey promptly. The level of miracles in your life will be directly related to your level of obedience. Faith without works is dead. You have an assignment, a destiny to fulfill.	
	6 am
	7 am
	8 am
	9 am
	10 am
	11 am
	12 pm
	1 pm
	2 pm
	3 pm
	4 pm
	5 pm
	6 pm
	7 pm
	8 pm
	9 pm

Date:

SCRIPTURE – DRAW CLOSER TO THE KING OF KINGS: Use your name in the place of a character in the scripture you're reading; imagine yourself in that time, using all 5 senses. Pray scripture back to God. Write the scripture down, read it, repeat it out loud throughout the day, memorize it, and meditate on it.

WORSHIP – PRAISE HIM FOR WHO HE IS: How will you glorify and magnify Him today? There is no room here for making personal petitions.

PURE HEART – ASK HIM TO PURIFY YOUR MIND AND HEART: Replace negative thoughts with higher thoughts. God's thoughts are noble, pure, lovely, excellent, right, true, and admirable. Ask God to reveal areas in your life that grieve the Holy Spirit. Confess with a contrite heart and receive forgiveness. As you confess, turn your palms up and release your sin, worry, and anxiety over to God. Now turn your palms down and receive God's love, mercy, favor, and grace.

THANKFULNESS – NAME THOSE THINGS YOU ARE THANKFUL FOR: There's always something to be grateful for. Name them one by one and come back often to rekindle the joy of each one of them.

O

O

O

O

O

O

O

REFLECTION & REVELATION – PRACTICE LISTENING FOR GOD: God promises that if you draw near to Him, He will tell you things you do not know. Who does God bring to mind? Where is God leading you? Reflect on God's perspective.	TASKS
PRAYER – YOU HAVE NOT BECAUSE YOU ASK NOT: Pray for family, friends, relationships, unity, community, world, church, favor, wisdom, God's will, work, and your future. Pray about anything and everything, without ceasing.	
OBEDIENCE – STAND, SHARE, SERVE: Take steps of faith, and obey promptly. The level of miracles in your life will be directly related to your level of obedience. Faith without works is dead. You have an assignment, a destiny to fulfill.	
	6 am
	7 am
	8 am
	9 am
	10 am
	11 am
	12 pm
	1 pm
	2 pm
	3 pm
	4 pm
	5 pm
	6 pm
	7 pm
	8 pm
	9 pm

Date:

SCRIPTURE – DRAW CLOSER TO THE KING OF KINGS: Use your name in the place of a character in the scripture you're reading; imagine yourself in that time, using all 5 senses. Pray scripture back to God. Write the scripture down, read it, repeat it out loud throughout the day, memorize it, and meditate on it.

WORSHIP – PRAISE HIM FOR WHO HE IS: How will you glorify and magnify Him today? There is no room here for making personal petitions.

PURE HEART – ASK HIM TO PURIFY YOUR MIND AND HEART: Replace negative thoughts with higher thoughts. God's thoughts are noble, pure, lovely, excellent, right, true, and admirable. Ask God to reveal areas in your life that grieve the Holy Spirit. Confess with a contrite heart and receive forgiveness. As you confess, turn your palms up and release your sin, worry, and anxiety over to God. Now turn your palms down and receive God's love, mercy, favor, and grace.

THANKFULNESS – NAME THOSE THINGS YOU ARE THANKFUL FOR: There's always something to be grateful for. Name them one by one and come back often to rekindle the joy of each one of them.

O

O

O

O

O

O

O

REFLECTION & REVELATION – PRACTICE LISTENING FOR GOD: God promises that if you draw near to Him, He will tell you things you do not know. Who does God bring to mind? Where is God leading you? Reflect on God's perspective.	TASKS
PRAYER – YOU HAVE NOT BECAUSE YOU ASK NOT: Pray for family, friends, relationships, unity, community, world, church, favor, wisdom, God's will, work, and your future. Pray about anything and everything, without ceasing.	
OBEDIENCE – STAND, SHARE, SERVE: Take steps of faith, and obey promptly. The level of miracles in your life will be directly related to your level of obedience. Faith without works is dead. You have an assignment, a destiny to fulfill.	
	6 am
	7 am
	8 am
	9 am
	10 am
	11 am
	12 pm
	1 pm
	2 pm
	3 pm
	4 pm
	5 pm
	6 pm
	7 pm
	8 pm
	9 pm

Date:

SCRIPTURE – DRAW CLOSER TO THE KING OF KINGS: Use your name in the place of a character in the scripture you're reading; imagine yourself in that time, using all 5 senses. Pray scripture back to God. Write the scripture down, read it, repeat it out loud throughout the day, memorize it, and meditate on it.

WORSHIP – PRAISE HIM FOR WHO HE IS: How will you glorify and magnify Him today? There is no room here for making personal petitions.

PURE HEART – ASK HIM TO PURIFY YOUR MIND AND HEART: Replace negative thoughts with higher thoughts. God's thoughts are noble, pure, lovely, excellent, right, true, and admirable. Ask God to reveal areas in your life that grieve the Holy Spirit. Confess with a contrite heart and receive forgiveness. As you confess, turn your palms up and release your sin, worry, and anxiety over to God. Now turn your palms down and receive God's love, mercy, favor, and grace.

THANKFULNESS – NAME THOSE THINGS YOU ARE THANKFUL FOR: There's always something to be grateful for. Name them one by one and come back often to rekindle the joy of each one of them.

O

O

O

O

O

O

O

REFLECTION & REVELATION – PRACTICE LISTENING FOR GOD: God promises that if you draw near to Him, He will tell you things you do not know. Who does God bring to mind? Where is God leading you? Reflect on God's perspective.	TASKS
PRAYER – YOU HAVE NOT BECAUSE YOU ASK NOT: Pray for family, friends, relationships, unity, community, world, church, favor, wisdom, God's will, work, and your future. Pray about anything and everything, without ceasing.	
OBEDIENCE – STAND, SHARE, SERVE: Take steps of faith, and obey promptly. The level of miracles in your life will be directly related to your level of obedience. Faith without works is dead. You have an assignment, a destiny to fulfill.	
	6 am
	7 am
	8 am
	9 am
	10 am
	11 am
	12 pm
	1 pm
	2 pm
	3 pm
	4 pm
	5 pm
	6 pm
	7 pm
	8 pm
	9 pm

Date:

SCRIPTURE – DRAW CLOSER TO THE KING OF KINGS: Use your name in the place of a character in the scripture you're reading; imagine yourself in that time, using all 5 senses. Pray scripture back to God. Write the scripture down, read it, repeat it out loud throughout the day, memorize it, and meditate on it.

WORSHIP – PRAISE HIM FOR WHO HE IS: How will you glorify and magnify Him today? There is no room here for making personal petitions.

PURE HEART – ASK HIM TO PURIFY YOUR MIND AND HEART: Replace negative thoughts with higher thoughts. God's thoughts are noble, pure, lovely, excellent, right, true, and admirable. Ask God to reveal areas in your life that grieve the Holy Spirit. Confess with a contrite heart and receive forgiveness. As you confess, turn your palms up and release your sin, worry, and anxiety over to God. Now turn your palms down and receive God's love, mercy, favor, and grace.

THANKFULNESS – NAME THOSE THINGS YOU ARE THANKFUL FOR: There's always something to be grateful for. Name them one by one and come back often to rekindle the joy of each one of them.

O

O

O

O

O

O

O

REFLECTION & REVELATION – PRACTICE LISTENING FOR GOD: God promises that if you draw near to Him, He will tell you things you do not know. Who does God bring to mind? Where is God leading you? Reflect on God's perspective.	TASKS
PRAYER – YOU HAVE NOT BECAUSE YOU ASK NOT: Pray for family, friends, relationships, unity, community, world, church, favor, wisdom, God's will, work, and your future. Pray about anything and everything, without ceasing.	
OBEDIENCE – STAND, SHARE, SERVE: Take steps of faith, and obey promptly. The level of miracles in your life will be directly related to your level of obedience. Faith without works is dead. You have an assignment, a destiny to fulfill.	
	6 am
	7 am
	8 am
	9 am
	10 am
	11 am
	12 pm
	1 pm
	2 pm
	3 pm
	4 pm
	5 pm
	6 pm
	7 pm
	8 pm
	9 pm

Date:

SCRIPTURE – DRAW CLOSER TO THE KING OF KINGS: Use your name in the place of a character in the scripture you're reading; imagine yourself in that time, using all 5 senses. Pray scripture back to God. Write the scripture down, read it, repeat it out loud throughout the day, memorize it, and meditate on it.

_____

_____

_____

_____

_____

_____

_____

_____

_____

_____

_____

_____

WORSHIP – PRAISE HIM FOR WHO HE IS: How will you glorify and magnify Him today? There is no room here for making personal petitions.

_____

_____

_____

PURE HEART – ASK HIM TO PURIFY YOUR MIND AND HEART: Replace negative thoughts with higher thoughts. God's thoughts are noble, pure, lovely, excellent, right, true, and admirable. Ask God to reveal areas in your life that grieve the Holy Spirit. Confess with a contrite heart and receive forgiveness. As you confess, turn your palms up and release your sin, worry, and anxiety over to God. Now turn your palms down and receive God's love, mercy, favor, and grace.

_____

_____

_____

THANKFULNESS – NAME THOSE THINGS YOU ARE THANKFUL FOR: There's always something to be grateful for. Name them one by one and come back often to rekindle the joy of each one of them.

O

O

O

O

O

O

O

REFLECTION & REVELATION – PRACTICE LISTENING FOR GOD: God promises that if you draw near to Him, He will tell you things you do not know. Who does God bring to mind? Where is God leading you? Reflect on God's perspective.	TASKS
PRAYER – YOU HAVE NOT BECAUSE YOU ASK NOT: Pray for family, friends, relationships, unity, community, world, church, favor, wisdom, God's will, work, and your future. Pray about anything and everything, without ceasing.	
OBEDIENCE – STAND, SHARE, SERVE: Take steps of faith, and obey promptly. The level of miracles in your life will be directly related to your level of obedience. Faith without works is dead. You have an assignment, a destiny to fulfill.	
	6 am
	7 am
	8 am
	9 am
	10 am
	11 am
	12 pm
	1 pm
	2 pm
	3 pm
	4 pm
	5 pm
	6 pm
	7 pm
	8 pm
	9 pm

Date:

SCRIPTURE – DRAW CLOSER TO THE KING OF KINGS: Use your name in the place of a character in the scripture you're reading; imagine yourself in that time, using all 5 senses. Pray scripture back to God. Write the scripture down, read it, repeat it out loud throughout the day, memorize it, and meditate on it.

WORSHIP – PRAISE HIM FOR WHO HE IS: How will you glorify and magnify Him today? There is no room here for making personal petitions.

PURE HEART – ASK HIM TO PURIFY YOUR MIND AND HEART: Replace negative thoughts with higher thoughts. God's thoughts are noble, pure, lovely, excellent, right, true, and admirable. Ask God to reveal areas in your life that grieve the Holy Spirit. Confess with a contrite heart and receive forgiveness. As you confess, turn your palms up and release your sin, worry, and anxiety over to God. Now turn your palms down and receive God's love, mercy, favor, and grace.

THANKFULNESS – NAME THOSE THINGS YOU ARE THANKFUL FOR: There's always something to be grateful for. Name them one by one and come back often to rekindle the joy of each one of them.

O

O

O

O

O

O

O

	TASKS
REFLECTION & REVELATION – PRACTICE LISTENING FOR GOD: God promises that if you draw near to Him, He will tell you things you do not know. Who does God bring to mind? Where is God leading you? Reflect on God's perspective.	
PRAYER – YOU HAVE NOT BECAUSE YOU ASK NOT: Pray for family, friends, relationships, unity, community, world, church, favor, wisdom, God's will, work, and your future. Pray about anything and everything, without ceasing.	
OBEDIENCE – STAND, SHARE, SERVE: Take steps of faith, and obey promptly. The level of miracles in your life will be directly related to your level of obedience. Faith without works is dead. You have an assignment, a destiny to fulfill.	
	6 am
	7 am
	8 am
	9 am
	10 am
	11 am
	12 pm
	1 pm
	2 pm
	3 pm
	4 pm
	5 pm
	6 pm
	7 pm
	8 pm
	9 pm

Printed in the United States
By Bookmasters